JAPANESE GARDENS

SAIHOJI GARDEN, KYOTO. Rocks in the pond symbolically represent trading ships anchored at night. Beautiful moss covers the ground, rocks and trees.

successor to *The Gardens of Japan*

JAPANESE
GARDENS *by* JIRO HARADA

CHARLES T. BRANFORD COMPANY
551 Boylston Street, Boston 16, Massachusetts

First published 1956

This book is copyright. It may not be reproduced in whole
or in part in any form without permission.
Application should be addressed to the publishers.

Published in London by The Studio Limited, 66 Chandos Place, W.C. 2
and in Boston, Massachusetts by the Charles T. Branford Company
Made and printed in England by William Clowes and Sons Limited, London and Beccles

CONTENTS AND ILLUSTRATIONS

PREFACE

Twenty-seven years ago my first volume *Gardens of Japan* was published by The Studio. During the quarter of a century that has elapsed since then the world has greatly changed and no country, perhaps, more than Japan. On the first anniversary of the day when World War II was brought to an end by his radio proclamation, at a ceremony held in the Palace garden, the Emperor is reported to have said: 'From now on let us concentrate on the building up of a magnificent nation devoted to cultural expansion.' Today, ten years later, Japan is more than ever resolved to contribute something worthwhile to the culture of the world.

Earlier this year one of my esteemed old friends in Europe wrote to me: 'The accelerating pace of our daily life with its noise and strain makes it increasingly necessary that we should have at hand a place of retreat for peace and meditation, and to me the Japanese garden would seem to provide such a setting which the West could adopt with much benefit. I should be very happy if the proposed book could open our eyes to the need for, and the value of rest and spiritual refreshment.'

It was largely in response to that call that I began preparing this book. First, I wanted to show my readers as many illustrations as possible which were not included in my former volume. This I was able to accomplish with a fair measure of success. But I found it most difficult to realize a second and far more important ambition—my desire to convey to them the feeling of peace and refreshment, of serenity, tranquillity and uplift which I have often felt when I gazed upon, or strolled in, the gardens which they illustrate. I soon realized that to get really adequate photographs would be very difficult. Nevertheless I persevered and have tried to show at least the historical background and something of the wealth and variety of gardens still preserved here even after the reckless destruction of war. Thus, though it leaves much to be desired, it is the hope of the author that this book will draw attention to the close approximation to the heart and spirit of the nature they love which our people have been able to reach in their gardens. This they were able to achieve by naturalistic, idealistic and symbolic means, not only with the art they have mastered during long centuries, but also by the help of various materials, particularly rocks, the appreciation of the stern quality and beauty of which would be of benefit to the world at large.

I wish to avail myself of this opportunity to express my sincere thanks to the Imperial Household authorities for granting me the privilege of taking photographs in the various Imperial gardens. My gratitude is due also to Professor Matsunosuke Tatsui and Mr Sanrei Shigemori for the valuable information contained in their authoritative works which much enlightened me in the preparation of this humble book.

JIRO HARADA
Tokyo, 1955

GENERAL OBSERVATIONS AND NOTES

1. HIDDEN IDEAS AND ULTIMATE AIM OF THE JAPANESE GARDEN

DURING its long history, extending over some 1300 years, the Japanese garden has developed many qualities. Some of them are obvious, others concealed; some based on traditions and superstitions, others on religious ideals.

The Shogun Yoshimasa (1435–90) was deeply fond of *ikebana* (flower arrangement) and gardens, and it was he who is generally believed to have brought 'auspicious' ideas into interior decorations and gardens. What was then known as an auspicious garden was a type of Horai landscape, centred on a rock composition representing the crane and the tortoise, symbols of long life, considered man's greatest happiness, the crane being traditionally believed to live one thousand, and the tortoise ten thousand, years.

Nothing has been so vitally connected with our gardens as this Horai, an imaginary island shaped like a tortoise in the ocean. It was an auspicious place believed to have been inhabited by cranes and tortoises as well as Immortals. This idea is generally traced to Chinese Taoism, and may have reached Japan quite early, for some believe that the Imperial burial mound with moats around it, established as early as the first century A.D., shows the influence of the Horai idea.

The idea of Shumisen, which was introduced into Japan with Buddhism, came to be mixed with that of Horai. It has its origin in Hindu cosmology and existed there before Buddhism took it over. It designated the central mountain of every world, of wonderful height and brilliancy. According to Hindu belief there was Indra's heaven or heavens at the top and around it eight circles of mountains and between them eight seas, the whole forming the nine mountains and eight seas constituting the universe.

At about the end of the Muromachi period or somewhat later the conventional representation of Horai as an island in the shape of a tortoise in a pond the shape of a crane in flight, became usual and from it must have developed later the garden with the rock composition of the crane and tortoise. As we have seen, this style of garden is thought by some to have started in the Momoyama period, but Professor Tatsui is of the opinion that it was created in the seventeenth century, in the Edo period.

There existed also in the Edo period the garden of pine, bamboo and plum (*Sho-chiku-bai*) a most auspicious group of plants used for decoration on happy occasions such as a wedding.

A grouping of seven, five and three rocks constitutes the Ryoanji garden; there is another in the garden of Shinjuan and perhaps also in the east garden of Daitokuji though the last has an extra rock. Its origin is not clear. Mr Shigemori traces it to rocks representing ships anchored in the water in a straight line as if on their way to or from Horai on a treasure-seeking expedition. When they are shown in a dry landscape, white sand represents water and rocks the ships. According to Mr Shigemori, these ships came to be represented by groups of seven, five and three stones and their origin was later forgotten.

They are the lucky odd numbers; seven is used in 'seven rare treasures', 'seven wise men of the bamboo thicket', and 'seven lucky gods', while five is the number associated with *gogyo* (the ancient conception of the five elementary forces, wood, fire, earth, metal and water, believed to be ever producing, and the same time ever destroying each other) and with *gojo* (five cardinal virtues—humanity, justice, politeness, wisdom and fidelity). Three is used in *sanyu* (three friends in the cold winter) or refers to the plum-tree, daffodil and bamboo, but this is a rather Chinese usage. These numbers are also those of the tufts of rice straw or paper which are twisted at fixed intervals in proper sequence in the rice-straw rope called *shime-nawa*, which is hung before shrines in order to sanctify the place within. *Shime-nawa* is often found tied around an aged tree or rock to indicate its sanctity.

With Taoism came the theory of *in* and *yo* which maintained that the universe was produced by the interaction of the male or positive (*yo*) and female or negative (*in*) principles. The association with the theory of numbers is that seven is unchangeable and appropriate to *yo*, five is a combination of *in* and *yo*, and three signifies heaven, earth and man. This theory is still applied to various forms of Japanese art including the garden. For instance, in planning artificial hills, if one is made rugged and precipitous and dynamic in mood, another will be smooth and serene, and static. If one waterfall gives the impression of masculine power, another should suggest feminine grace. If there is a peninsula projecting into the lake, there should be a bay to counterbalance it. In laying out stepping stones, if a concave-shaped stone is used, it should be followed by one with a projection. Beside a large rock standing erect, there should generally be a low reclining one. The principle of positive and negative is applied to the layout, to the selection of materials, and also to the details of construction.

Christianity, first brought into Japan by St Francis Xavier in 1549, and prohibited in 1589, has also left its mark on Japanese gardens, especially with the stone lantern of Oribe type. Oribe was a convert to Christianity and Rikyu's disciple in the tea ceremony. He originated the design of a stone lantern with a pillar suggesting a cross and a carving of the Virgin Mary further down. When Christianity was placed under the government this was replaced by Jizo, a Buddhist deity. The Oribe type of stone lantern is still widely used in Japanese gardens.

Needless to say our gardens have also been strongly influenced by Buddhism. This was quite natural as many eminent Buddhist priests have taken an active interest in garden construction and have designed a number of famous gardens which are preserved to this day. Indeed nearly every great temple in Japan has an excellent garden carefully preserved in spite of being often several centuries old. Yet I have found that Buddhistic elements in Japanese gardens have in the main been submerged under other conventions, traditions and superstitions. Take for instance the waterfall, which is said to be a symbolic representation of Fudo Myoo (Sanskrit, *Acala*). This deity is the messenger of the Buddha, being the chief of the five Myoo (Raja). He is represented in painting and sculpture with a fierce mien overawing all evil spirits. He carried a sharp wisdom-sword and a noose. His hair falls over his left shoulder and he usually stands or sits on a rock, one eye half-closed, the other wide open, or with one looking up and the other down, mouth shut, teeth gripping upper lip, and forehead wrinkled. He is usually represented against a flaming nimbus and is generally attended by boys, two or eight in number. There is no apparent connection between Fudo and waterfalls and since his image is neither used nor suggested, few ordinary persons will be reminded of this fierce-looking Raja by merely gazing upon a waterfall composed of rocks and water, yet the symbol is traditionally there.

Among others, the Rakan (*Arhats* or Buddhist saints) are also suggested in gardens, such as in the one belonging to Ikkyuji. In that garden a group of sixteen Rakan is represented merely by natural rocks. There are no marks of identification except that the rocks, of varying sizes, are in sixteen groups. Rakan are generally represented as either 16 or 500 in number.

Again, some rocks in the garden are placed in a group which traditionally suggests a Buddhist Trinity with Amida in the middle, attended by two deities, one of Mercy and the other of Wisdom. But having no identification marks—and in all Buddhistic images, either in painting or sculpture, the main mark of identification is the *mudra* (the way they hold their hands and fingers)—they are not distinguishable from the Shakamuni Trinity or any other. This was presumably of little importance to garden planners. Their aim may have been to produce a pleasing group of rocks expressing aesthetic principles by means of harmony of lines or balance of masses. Yet the ideal of the great garden masters such as Soami, when they designed Japanese gardens, seems to have been to re-create a landscape and infuse it with spiritual values so that the garden might represent the Mandara (expressing the mystic doctrine of the two realms, one the principle and cause, the other the intelligence and the effect) in Amida's Paradise in the West.

One thing must be noted in this connection, that it does not seem that priests in general regarded these rocks as images of deities; rather they tried to express aesthetic principles by means of the Buddhistic doctrines with which the people were more or less familiar.

Nevertheless designers of Japanese gardens try to infuse the spirit of nature into the creations. They still strive to suggest a sylvan solitude or seaside tranquillity, the grandeur of a tremendous gorge or the sublimity of a mighty river, the rhythmic contour of undulating hills or the peaceful expanse of a plain or a vast stretch of water. In short they try to make the garden a place in which men may commune with nature.

Moreover, garden designers try to avoid being too ostentatious. Beautiful objects should be so concealed that only those who seek diligently may find them and thus be thrilled with unexpected joy, even as men should do kind deeds to others in secret, to be found out by accident, if at all.

I remember some years ago I visited a half-finished garden near Okazaki Park in Kyoto which contained some beautiful groups of rocks, especially one group of three, marvellously well composed. So beautifully was each rock shaped and so well placed was the group that it gave a definite character to that garden. These rocks projecting out of the ground, looked so firm and strong that they appeared like an immense rocky outcrop on the mountain side revealed by centuries of natural erosion, and created the atmosphere of a wild mountain suitable as a background for two ancient trees planted there. Unfortunately, it so happened that the residence for which the garden was being constructed had to be taken down, and the garden, which was not quite finished, had to be abandoned. Accordingly, that part of the garden which included the admirable group of rocks was dug up, and it was a revelation to me to find that these rocks, none of which projected more than two feet above the ground, were really each five or six feet in height, with more than two-thirds of the mass buried under the ground. For the first time I saw why these rocks carried such weight in the garden, since the suggestion of latent strength under the ground invested them with their dominating power. It was a sort of moral force deriving its strength from sacrifice made in silence.

Following this line of thought let me recount what the great tea-master Rikyu did more than 360 years ago in order to give his garden a deep spiritual significance. When his new tea-room and garden were completed at Sakai he invited a few of his friends to a tea ceremony for the house-warming. Knowing the greatness of Rikyu, the guests who accepted the invitation naturally expected to find some ingenious design for his garden which would make the best use of the view of the sea, the house being on the slope of a hill. But when they arrived they were amazed to find that a number of large evergreen trees had been planted on one side of the garden, evidently to obstruct the view of the sea. They were at a loss to understand the meaning of this. Later when the time came for the guests to enter the tea-room, they proceeded one by one over the stepping-stones in the garden to the stone water-basin to rinse their mouths and wash their hands, a gesture of symbolic cleansing, physically and mentally, before entering the tea-room. Then it was found that when a guest stooped to scoop out a dipperful of water from the water-basin, only in that humble posture was he suddenly able to get a glimpse of the shimmering sea in the distance by way of an opening through the trees, thus making him realize the relationship between the dipperful of water in his hand and the great ocean beyond, and also enabling him to recognize his own position in the universe; he was thus brought into a correct relationship with the Infinite.

Aesthetics may require a garden to be something more than a reproduction of nature. But if a garden does really re-create nature, though on a small scale, will it not be possible for it to inspire and uplift us as the grandeur of nature does?

I quote from Mr Schellbach's admirable articles recently published in *The National Geographic Magazine*, 'As always during my many trips over Bright Angel and other trails, I experienced an uplifting of the spirit combined with a deep sense of humility as our party started down into the incredible chasm.' In a somewhat different way, did not Rikyu's garden at Sakai give to the guests on that day a similar pleasure: something profound, a spark from heaven that enlightens our soul? I too have more than once experienced that uplifting of the spirit combined with a deep sense of humility during my many visits to the Grand Canyon of Arizona and the Yosemite.

I once spent a moonlight night at the bottom of that mile-deep canyon and was fascinated to watch the ever-changing shadows of the pinnacles as the moon crossed the canyon. Many times have I stood on the bank of the Mirror Lake in the Yosemite Valley at dawn and watched the marvellous reflection of the sky on the water until the sun began peeping out from behind the Half Dome; I have prolonged my enjoyment of the first glimpse of the sun's reflection for a whole minute by slowly moving along the bank of the lake. Rare experiences like this have been more than once awakened in my mind while in a Japanese garden. Even though it may be with a stretch of imagination, would it not be possible for us to see the dawn gilding 'islands in the sky' and leaving canyons in blue shadow? Would not evening set the earth's spires alight with alpen-glow, or let moonlight tint the chasm with mystery, and morning's fog, if it came, fill the canyon with a river of cotton?

It seems to be within our make-up that many of us do not get complete satisfaction from the beauty of nature as it is. We love the beauty of nature to be sure, but we want to go a little further. We like to regenerate that beauty by symbolizing or idealizing it. Of course the beauty of nature may be enjoyed subjectively as well as objectively. If it is enjoyed merely objectively, and the desire is lacking to re-create it or express it in some other form, is not our enjoyment less vital than when this desire is present?

The gardens of Japan, it may be said, have been developed by man's intense admiration of nature. They have given him great enjoyment and led him to love nature more. As a result, gardens were made as epitomes of nature, by men motivated by the desire to re-create nature in accordance with its ways and spirit, or revivify it by symbolic or idealistic means.

It seems the people of the Far East have been endowed with an inborn love of landscapes.

In general they have a strong love for profound and tranquil landscapes. To them the only source of poetic inspiration is to be found in nature.

To be sure, in great antiquity, nature itself was the object of worship, it being part and parcel of the whole religion. There was a time when our people looked upon a forest as the god himself or as his shrine. In the *Manyoshu* (our eighth-century anthology) the word *jinsha*, now meaning shrine, was made to read *mori* (forest).

Forests were regarded as identical with the abode of gods and some places are so even today, as in the case of Kanasana Jinsha in Musashi Province. There is no real shrine behind the place of worship: only a forest. There are two other such places I know of: one is Suwa Jinsha in Nagano Prefecture, and the other Omiwa Jinsha in Yamato Province, where the forest of Miwa mountain is still regarded as the shrine. No wonder that our people have been greatly influenced by nature, so much so that they wanted to enjoy it as their own. From this desire has resulted the creation and development of the art of landscape gardening, ever striving to re-create nature in one form or another, be it in symbols or idealism.

2. GENERAL PLAN OF JAPANESE HILL-TYPE GARDENS

All important books on our gardens published in Japan since the fifteenth century contain a drawing such as the one illustrated here, showing the fundamental principles guiding the layout of a hill garden.

These fundamental principles are still generally followed, though of course the details of layout have changed from time to time with styles and ideals.

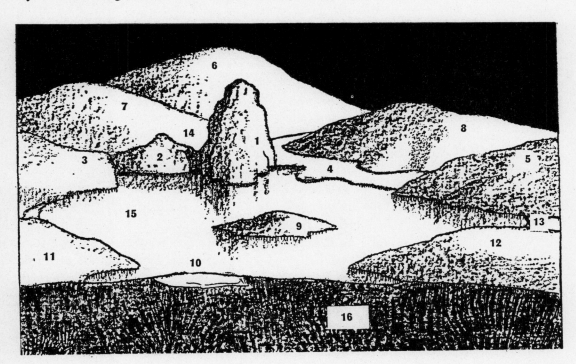

1 guardian stone	5 near mountain	9 central island	13 lake outlet
2 small hill for cascade	6 distant mountain	10 worshipping stone	14 cascade mouth
3 side mountain	7 middle mountain	11 master's island	15 lake
4 sand-blown beach	8 mountain spur	12 guest's island	16 broad beach

13

From the Nara period (645–781) to the Late Heian (898–1185) Japanese gardens were generally large, and contained a large pond with three or four islands in it. This Horai island generally lay along the front of the symmetrically-built mansion which had pavilions jutting out into the pond.

From the end of the Kamakura (1186–1333) to the Yoshinocho period (1334–1393) the pond was shaped somewhat like the Chinese character for 'heart' and the garden was laid usually in two levels. Similarly-shaped ponds continued to be made into the period that followed.

From the Muromachi (1394–1572) to the Momoyama period (1573–1602) dry landscape gardens came into fashion with the influence of the Zen sect of Buddhism. The majority of gardens of this period had no real pond but a rectangular area in front of the *shoin* or in a right-angled shape along the two sides of the *shoin*; in these areas a dry landscape garden was laid.

In the Early Edo period (1603–1680) the pond came to be made generally in the shape of an ornate form of the Chinese character for water. From the Middle Edo period (1681–1778), however, the use of the hillside again came into vogue and the garden was made in two levels; the pond became long, and no longer in the shape of the character for 'heart' or 'water'.

In olden times some gardens were viewed from a boat in the pond and those made from the Late Heian to Kamakura periods were called *Chisen-shuyu-shiki* (garden with pond to be enjoyed from a boat). The gardens of the Yoshinocho period were viewed by boat as well as by sauntering along the garden paths. From the Muromachi through the Momoyama and into the Early Edo period the gardens were of the type known as *Chisen-kaiyu-shiki* (garden with pond to be appreciated by sauntering) in which paths were laid around the pond. After the Early Edo period the garden had a pond, but was so planned as to be best enjoyed from a given point in the house, as is indicated by the name *Chisen-kansho-shiki*.

Soon after the Restoration of 1868 gardens with large ponds again came to be made, but unlike those of the Late Heian period they were so planned as to be enjoyed by walking along the paths around the pond, instead of by boat.

It may be mentioned here that Japanese gardens have long been classified, according to the character of the ground, into two general types; *tsuki-yama* (artificial hills) and *hira-niwa* (level gardens), the vicissitudes of the past 1300 years or so having developed some special features in each. As the names signify, the former consists of hills and ponds, while the latter makes use of a flat piece of ground to represent generally a valley or a moor. To be sure the two are not always inseparable: the former, if it is a considerable size, may give up a part of itself to make a *hira-niwa*.

The use of stepping stones, stone lanterns and *tsukubai* (stone water-basins for washing hands prior to entering the *chaseki*) started after *roji* path gardens became a fashion in the Momoyama period along with the development of *chanoyu* and *chaseki*. We find these objects in some gardens of the pre-Momoyama period, but only where that part has been added or modified later.

1   2   3   4

3. CLASSIFICATION AND GROUPING OF ROCKS

In constructing gardens according to the traditional style, rocks are grouped into five classes according to their shape. The first is called *reisho-seki* (rock of symbolical or spiritual form), standing upright with massive base and tapering top, and often used for the guardian rock of the garden, as it symbolizes the Great Ultimate in which positive and negative unite. The second is *taizo-seki* (body-rock) which is tall and somewhat bulging in the middle, and is often used in the construction of a waterfall. The third is *shintai-seki* (heart-rock) which is flat. The fourth is *shikei-seki* (branching rock) which has a prominent projection. The fifth is *kikyaku-seki* (reclining rock) which is recumbent.

5

The five rocks may be grouped in different ways by varying the position of the rocks. Below are given three examples in grouping, each of which may create a beautiful spot complete in itself, in any corner of the garden.

Five in a group.
ormal style of Three Powers.

Five in a group.
Armour style composition
in a garden in Osaka.

Five in a group.
Tranquillity style composition.

c

b

a

d

e

The rocks may be grouped in eight combinations of three as follows:

a. *Rei-shin-kyaku-gumi* (spiritual-heart-reclining combination): rock of spiritual form combined with heart-rock and reclining rock. These are used in all sorts of places.

b. *Reiyo-kyaku-gumi* (spirit-positive and reclining combination): rock of spiritual form, combined with branching-rock and reclining rock. May be used in various places.

c. *Reido-kyaku-gumi* (spirit-body-reclining combination): rock of symbolical or spiritual form and body-rock combined with reclining rock. Used on the waist of the hill, at the waterfall, and at the root of trees.

d. *Rei-shi-shin-gumi* (rock of spiritual form and branching rock combined with heart-rock). To be used at the waist of the hill.

e. *Rei-shin-do-gumi* (rock of spiritual form and heart rock combined with body-rock) . . . This combination is also known as *Getsu-in-seki-gumi* (moon-shadow-rock combination). Generally used in such a way as to be seen beyond a hill.

f. *Rei-shi-do-gumi* (rock of spiritual form and branching rock combined with body-rock): used at a waterfall, along a steep road or on the middle island. The combination is also called *Taki-zoe-gumi* (a composition to be added to a waterfall).

g. *Shin-shi-tai-gumi* (heart and branching rocks combined with body-rock): used on the middle island and at the foot of hills.

h. *Shin-tai-kyaku-gumi* (heart- and body-rocks. combined with reclining rock): (widely used, also being known as *Nio-gumi* two *deva* kings combination).

f

g

h

16

I   2   3   4

These rocks may be grouped in twos in ten combinations, each called by a different name as follows:

1. *Reisho-gumi* (spiritual-first combination): rock of spiritual form combined with heart-rock. Suitable for the top or hip of the hill, or on the plain or, in fact, almost anywhere.

2. *Rei-eki-gumi* (combination of spiritual changes): rock of spiritual form combined with branching rock. Suitable for hills or water's edge.

3. *Shin-shin-gumi* (heart-fidelity combination): heart-rock combined with reclining rock. May be used anywhere.

4. *Futai-gumi* (wind-conceived combination): body-rock combined with branching rock. Known as the watchful combination; used at the water's edge but not on the plain.

5. *Reikyaku-gumi* (courtesy-reclining combination): body-rock combined with reclining rock. Effective under trees.

6. *Shikyaku-gumi* (branching-reclining combination): branching rock combined with reclining rock.

7. *Niso-gumi* (double-feature combination): rock of spiritual form combined with body-rock. Used on the top or hip of the hill, under trees or many other places.

8. *Shutai-gumi* (principal conception combination): rock of spiritual form combined with reclining rock. This may be used in many places with effect.

9. *Shorei-gumi* (first spiritual combination): branching rock combined with heart-rock. Two views of this group are given. Usually used at the water's edge.

10. *Futai-gumi* (wind-body combination): heart-rock combined with body-rock. Used to help trees and plants.

5

6

10   9   8   7

There are many books in Japan purporting to contain valuable secrets concerning the art of garden-making. When technical knowledge came to be required in making gardens, especially after the Kamakura and Muromachi periods, specialists and books of this type were in demand.

While many of these so-called 'secrets' may be regarded today as worthless, there are some which contain valuable truths that may be of use to those who are interested in gardens. Below will be found a few excerpts from well-known sources; some of them may interest my readers.

From *Sakutei-ki* (Notes on Making Gardens) by Gokyogoku Yoshitsune, who was killed in 1206 at the age of 38.

'The waterfall symbolizes Fudo Myoo. When a waterfall is three or four feet high it represents Fudo. Therefore there should be two rocks representing his two boy attendants.

'In a landscape garden, earth represents the Emperor, the water his subjects. Water flows wherever earth allows it, and when earth obstructs, the water will stop flowing. It is also said that the mountain represents the Emperor, and water his subjects, with the rocks as vassals, supporting the Emperor. Water flows as willed by the mountain, but when the mountain is weak, the water will destroy the mountain. The weakness of the mountain is due to the lack of strength in the rocks supporting it.

'Rocks at the base of the mountain and in the fields should be like shaggy dogs lying, or like a group of pigs scattering, or like calves disporting themselves with their mother.

'It should be borne in mind that if there is a stone or two suggestive of running, there should be seven or eight suggestive of pursuit.

'If a rock is erected in the garden, it should be made to stand strong. That does not mean it must be planted deep in the ground, for even if it is deeply planted, it may seem weak if too isolated.

'A rock should be carefully considered before it is erected. Once it is put upright, it should not be laid down, and vice versa. To do so will irritate the spirit of the rock and do harm to its owner.

'The pond should be dug in the shape of a crane or tortoise. The water follows the shape of the container.'

From *Saga-ryu Niwa Koho Hiden no Sho* (Secret Old Laws in Making Saga-style Gardens), copied first in 1395 by Yasuhira (probably an imaginary name). It gives a sketch of a plan of a hill garden showing different hills, including Guest Island, Host Island and Middle Island in the pond, worshipping stone, beach, etc.

'The first essential in laying out a landscape garden is the preparation of a plan. The design of the landscape should be set out in the plan.

'Then rocks should be erected, trees planted, thus creating a scene. According to the space available, some hills, islands, or rocks may be left out.'

From *Tsukiyama Teizo-den* (Making of Hill Gardens) by Soami, who died in 1525.

'Those who are desirous of becoming experts should make sketches of surpassing scenes whenever and wherever they find them. They should not fail to make notes and be able to picture to themselves the view whenever they wish to reproduce it. If they should discipline themselves in this manner, they will naturally become expert.

'However small the garden may be, it can be made to include high mountains many miles away, and to create waterfalls of tremendous height. There is a method of including distant waters and the vast expanse of the ocean. All this is possible by knowing how to handle water and rocks.

'The ultimate aim of the landscape garden is to reveal the mysteries of nature and creation. This may be achieved by a simple flat garden with only a few rocks. However interesting may be the pattern and beautiful the scenes, the truth of the hills may be lost and even the heart of the master may appear ignoble, if the garden is lacking in coherence and incomplete in construction.

'Everything in this universe is correlated. This is a natural law preordained. When one is about to make a garden, one should not be absorbed merely by the pattern, or carelessly plant even one tree or place one rock without careful discrimination.

'*Honsho ribetsu* should be avoided; that is to say, a plant which grows in the heart of a high mountain should not be planted by the pond, or a plant which grows by the water should not be planted on the hill-top.

'Distant mountains appear low and when they are nearby, they appear high. Distant waterfalls appear high, and nearby ones look low. These facts must be borne in mind when constructing a landscape garden.

'All the landscapes represent Mandara of the nine realms of Amida's Pure Land. Therefore, every rock used in the garden stands for either Buddha, Bodhisattva or Raja. All the mountains, islands and plains are manifestations of the nine realms of the Pure Land. Therefore Buddhas and Bodhisattvas are manifested wherever there is a landscape.

'The presence of stones representing a trinity marks the place to be *Jomon Josho* (upper superior), where the highest type of incarnate being is found, this being the highest of the nine stages of birth in the Pure Land.

'There are other deities—twelve *devas*, especially of the Shingon sect: Brahma the *deva* of earth, of the moon, of the sun; Indra, of Fire; Yama, of the Raksas (or demons) of water, of wind; Vaisramana (wealth); and Mahesvara (Siva). Twenty-eight *shuku*; 28 heavens or *devalokas*; 6 of the desire world, 18 of the form world, 4 *arupa* or formless heavens.

'Landscape presents five elements: earth, water, fire, wind and sky. Earth consists of mountains and islands. Water is ocean. Fire is manifested by flowers. It is the wind which opens flowers and scatters them. Sky is suggested by the blue of various plants and grasses. Sky—blue; wind—white; fire—red; water—black; earth—yellow. *Go-jo* (five cardinal virtues); *jin* (humanity), *gi* (justice), *rei* (politeness), *chi* (wisdom), *shin* (fidelity).

'The Chinese poet Pai-lo-t'ien made a small pond in his garden and planted some bamboo on its bank because he loved bamboo. He thought that bamboo had nothing inside to conceal, so it was good for him to have it for his friend. He also had a little stream, for he loved water because its nature was pure, so that he wanted it for his teacher. He kept

19

himself free from worldly desires and remained pure and unspoiled, enjoying himself with poems and songs. He found nourishment in the water of the spring. Men such as he are true lovers of nature and may indeed be called amiable persons. If a man can be awakened from drowsiness and be led to the righteous path by looking upon a landscape, there is something precious in him. Being righteous is inseparable from the love of landscape.

'Even in a limited area, a landscape suggestive of the heart of a mountain or deep ravine can be created, but only by an expert. Take for instance the case of a waterfall. If a waterfall is exposed to a full view from the top to the bottom, it will appear low and add very little to the scenic effect. But if the upper part of it be concealed by trees, the middle part partially hidden by a projecting rock or by a branch of a tree and the basin have a growth of grass or plants, then the fall is not exposed in its entirety, and may give the impression of being of a great height. It is the same with the pond. If it is large and square and has nothing to hide any part of it, one can see it all at a glance, and nothing is left to the imagination. Whereas the pond may be small but, with winding contours, partly concealed by trees or rocks, it may give us an impression of a large lake or a bay that might afford a glimpse of an expanse of sea beyond. It requires an ability to express and understand the secrets of nature.

'Too great a stress cannot be placed on the importance of the dignity or the spiritual quality of the nature represented. Caution should be taken not to be too anxious to over-crowd the scenery to make it more interesting. Such an effort often results in a loss of dignity and a falling into vulgarity. One's heart and mind should be concentrated on the profundity of nature, and there should not be any suspicion of frivolity in one's attitude towards it.

'When making a garden it may be necessary to lower a hill within the garden, or cut down certain trees so as to take in distant views and establish a proper relationship with the surrounding scenery.

'When a real tea-master lays out a garden he will try to conceal his art so that his work may look natural, and to create a deep forest or valley even if the place may be surrounded by city dwelling-houses.'

1. PRE-KAMAKURA PERIOD (-1183)

PRE-BUDDHISTIC PERIOD (-552)

JAPAN is blessed by beautiful natural scenery, and so from earliest times her people have been born and nurtured in beautiful surroundings. The Japanese have sought to heighten this beauty and profundity of nature in their gardens so that they have become a living art, developed on unique lines. Therein is their essence.

It is interesting to observe how close were the thoughts of the people to the beauty and truth revealed by nature as shown in their records and verses left to us. Our *Kojiki* (published in A.D. 712) and *Nihon Shoki* (earliest Japanese history, published in A.D. 720) both describe the creation, the birth of the first god, as the putting forth of a young shoot from a reed in the mud. Another instance is given by our national anthem which may be roughly rendered:

> 'May our August reign last
> for ever and ever
> Until the pebbles grow into moss-covered rocks'

The words were taken from a 31-syllabled verse in the *Kokinshu*, an anthology of 1,111 verses chosen in A.D. 905 by Imperial command by four great poets of the time.

The idea of Horai already existed in the reign of Suinin Tenno (29 B.C.–A.D. 70) when the Imperial Palace was built on an island in the lake in the garden. The idea may be even older, for it is recorded that the palace was built on an island surrounded by water in the reign of Sujin Tenno.

It had long existed in China for Shih Huang Ti, who became the king of Ch'in in 246 B.C., in his search for the Elixir of Life, was told that in the eastern sea there were three sacred mountains Horai, Hojo, and Eishu, where many immortals were said to live. It is recorded in Chinese history that Huang Ti had several large ships built, loaded them with gold, silver, jewels, grains and other precious articles and with hundreds of chaste boys and maidens, and sent Ch'u Fu with them in search of Horai to obtain this Elixir. Ch'u Fu arrived at Kumano in Kii province in Japan in 219 B.C., in the reign of Korei Tenno. Being unable to find the Elixir of Life, and afraid of the possible consequences, he did not return to China. His tomb-stone now stands at Shingu at the mouth of the Kumano River to tell the sad end of his search.

The feast of the winding stream conducted in a garden was started in Japan in the reign of Sujin Tenno (97–30 B.C.) and it became a fashion in the court as a literary entertainment.

Stones sometimes symbolically represented gods. Rocks in groups of three were used in gardens either at the waterfall, or for worshipping stones and after the advent of Buddhism, the trinity of Amida or Shaka.

ASUKA PERIOD (552–644)

The Horai idea had already come from China, and Buddhism was officially introduced into Japan from Korea in 552.

Not only the first garden plan, but also the first gardeners, presumably came from Korea.

SITE OF THE IMPERIAL GARDEN OF OSAWA POND, SAGA. The Imperial garden at Saga was laid out for the villa established by Emperor Saga who reigned from 809 and died here twenty years after he had abdicated the throne in 822.

This is the oldest site in Japan of an Imperial garden, and it may be regarded as the first garden in Japan. The area of the site is nearly 15 acres, and it is important, not only historically, but also from the point of style and technique.

Protected by a range of mountains at the back to the north, and with an open view to the south stretching to distant hills to the west, the large pond of Osawa was an ideal spot for a villa and a garden. It was in 879 that this important villa, together with many of its buildings and the garden, was turned into a Buddhist temple, and was named Daigaku-ji, which continues to thrive and has done much to preserve the pond and principal features of the original garden.

Saga Tenno was known for his scholarly attainment and poetic achievements, as well as his artistic interests. He often assembled poets here and encouraged them in their work. He frequently held parties here to enjoy the beauties of nature at the moon-viewing and for appreciation of snow views. A tradition has it that one day he went out in a boat in the Osawa pond and gathered a few chrysanthemums growing on Kikujima, one of the two islands. These flowers he later arranged in a vase which symbolically represented the heaven, earth and man in their proper relations. He was greatly pleased with the arrangement and is reported to have recommended to others in the palace to follow the example and perpetuate the principles involved. The Saga school of flower arrangement now has millions of followers throughout the country, and the Daigaku-ji temple maintains an exclusive school in its compound and issues diplomas.

There is a group of several rocks firmly composed and standing at about half-way between the two islands in the pond. Though this is the only group now usually visible above the water, there are four other groups arranged more or less in a straight line along the south side of Tenjin island, all being immersed in water now. These five groups of rocks evidently stood for Yotomari-seki, which symbolically represented ships anchored at night in a harbour on their way to Horai-jima in quest of treasures or on their way home loaded with treasures. It was customary for the gardens of the eighth and ninth centuries to have such a feature introduced, and the custom continued through the Kamakura into the Muromachi period.

In the Kamakura period, the Osawa pond came to be used as a reservoir for irrigating paddy-fields cultivating rice. This necessitated a change in the southern half of the pond where it was made much deeper, some places being as deep as 13 feet. The northern half of the pond still preserves the original bottom which had been hardened with a quantity of coarse sand and gravel so as to keep the water clear, which was essential for the enjoyment of the boat-ride: it was no more than 3 feet deep as was the custom of the time for the sake of safety.

23

It is reported that a man from Kudara (Korea), named Shikimaro, had a body all mottled with white and he was about to be thrown into the sea. But he begged for his life, saying he was able to construct a mountain with rocks. His life was saved, and he was given a chance to show his skill. Thereupon, he constructed a mountain in the south garden of the palace. What he made was a symbolic Shumisen built of rocks on the island in the garden lake. An arching bridge was also constructed to connect the island with the mainland.

According to the description given, the Shumisen was surrounded by a steep precipice. Some Buddhist figures as well as images of Taoist immortals, were placed together showing a combination of the two religions.

Umako laid out a garden close to the Asuka River having many islands in the lake, and he was therefore called *Shima daijin* (minister of islands).

About this time Shotoku Taishi too laid out a garden for the Jorinji temple. Thus in the Asuka period Taoistic Horai-zan and Buddhist Shumisen were symbolically represented by a rock composition or by an artificial mound.

In both cases there was a middle island, connected to the mainland by an arching bridge. There also existed crane islands and tortoise islands.

THE NARA PERIOD (645–782)

In this period poems on the feasts of the winding stream were composed by men of letters. The eighth-century anthology of poetry called the *Man-yoshu* contains some verses written on plum blossom for such an occasion, and another which the Emperor ordered to be composed when he felt regret at seeing plum blossom fall. Gardens of that time also contained *yamabuki* (Kerria japonica), as well as wisteria and hagi (*Lespedeza bicolor*). Bamboo gardens also existed for there is a verse referring to one. A lotus pond festival is also known to have taken place, and people enjoyed themselves among the hills and by the seashore as may be gathered from such a quotation as the following:

'Gazing at the mountain one's knowledge is widened; looking upon the water one's feeling of benevolence is increased.'

During this period the two types of gardens already mentioned gradually developed into natural scenic gardens. Generally speaking, they were large and were enjoyed by means of a boat. The stones in a Horai composition had been vertical, while those in a Shumisen composition were slanting, but already in this period the two seem to have become confused and it no longer mattered whether a Shumisen type was adopted for a palace garden or a Horai type for a temple garden.

HEIAN PERIOD (784–1183)

There was considerable development in the garden-maker's art in this period, more care was taken in the selection of a site, and it became fashionable for large gardens to be attached to mansions of princes and noblemen.

The Shosei-en was laid out by Minamoto-no Tooru. It represented the district of Shiogama with its salt pans. The pond had four islands; one represented Horai-zan; and two others, the crane and tortoise islands, still remain and retain some of original rock composition.

According to the *Honcho Bunsui* under the date of 10th month, 5th year Tengen (982) the

JINSEN-EN, KYOTO, near Nijo Palace. The Jinsen-en ('sacred fountain garden') is recorded in Japanese history as having been laid out when Kyoto was established as the capital of Japan in 794. Imperial boating parties were held in this garden and so was the 'feast of the winding stream' (*Kyokusui no en*), which was a literary pastime much favoured by the Court of the time. Cups filled with wine were floated down the winding stream and the guests, seated along the edge of the water, picked them up and drank while composing poems on a given subject.

This garden is described as having been very spacious. Dragons were believed to live in its lake and this gave rise to many legends. Here, at a time of drought, the famous Kobo Daishi is said to have prayed to the dragons for rain. The garden has gradually dwindled until now there remains only a fraction of the original lake with a small island in it. Shinto shrines have preserved the sanctity of the site and it is said that Takenouchi Seiho, a famous Kyoto painter in the traditional style, who lived near the garden and died only a few years ago, came here to pray whenever he started a new painting.

25

mansion of the time was enclosed by a fence with a gate. In making gardens a higher place would be made into an artificial hill and a lower one into a pond; a small edifice on the west side of the pond should be erected for Buddhist images, and a small palace erected on the east side of the pond for study or for wife and children to live. 40 per cent of the whole area should be given to the buildings, 30 per cent to the garden, and 30 per cent for vegetation. The garden should have islands with green pines and white sandy beaches. In the water there should be red carps, and on the land white herons : there should be a small bridge, and a small boat.

In 902 when he was to be exiled to Dazaifu in Kyushu, Michizane composed the following verse to the plum-tree in his garden close to the Gojobo gate in Kyoto :

> When the east wind blows send me your fragrance.
> Forget not the Spring even though your master may be away.

When the ex-emperor Uda had a moon-viewing party in his garden the subject given to the assembled poets was 'The Shadow of the Moon filling the Autumn Pond.'

The Tale of Genji mentions the voices of insects and the flight of fireflies as attractions in a garden and refers to the importance of rocks in gardens in the chapter entitled 'Akashi.'

Garden lovers of this period appreciated the beauty of flowing water, and when there was no moon, they lighted lanterns along the streams. They felt it was essential to view gardens from boats and the water in ponds was three feet, more or less, in depth the bottom being hardened with clay and pebbles, for it was necessary to have clear water in order to enjoy boating.

Some rock formations of the famous cataract of 'Nakoso' at Saga, Kyoto, still remain close to the pond of Osawa originally of the detached imperial palace of Saga Tenno, and now in the garden of the Daigaku-ji. There also remain some stones in the pond representing ships anchored at night; others used on the crane and tortoise islands also remain to this day. Later three different rocks were used, often with a space between them, in forming a triad, but in this period they were generally grouped close together, thus giving an appearance sometimes of a single rock with three peaks.

Rock compositions, especially those of the late Heian period, suggest latent power. In the Nara period it was fashionable to reproduce some famous scene on a small scale but in the Heian period gardens assumed a more or less fixed style and showed a tendency to become formal.

For the Imperial palace or the homes of aristocrats the form of architecture was generally *shinden-Zukuri* in which buildings were arranged more or less symmetrically with two structures jutting out into the pond where there was one and the different buildings connected by corridors.

KANJU-JI GARDEN, suburb of KYOTO. This is the site of Miyamichi's manor-house, which had a garden renowned even in the ninth century, when the creation of gardens was quite the vogue. It was later the site for the Buddhist temple of Kanju-ji which is still maintained. Judging from the description left by an official from Po Hai who happened to pass by, the garden was suggestive of Horai jima, a fairyland where immortals are said to dwell.

During the Kamakura (1186–1333) and Muromachi (1394–1572) periods, Kanju-ji garden was famous for plum blossoms. There is a diary showing that two days were spent in clearing water-weeds from the pond in June 1660.

Judging from what now remains, the original garden may not have been much larger than it is today, about 5¼ acres. Kanjuji must have been typical of a water garden of the day, to be appreciated by boating on the pond, which contained four or five islets suggestive of Elysium.

The stone lantern with arching roof which is famous as the Kanju-ji type, came to be made in the late Edo period.

When the pond was cleaned some years ago, gravel was inadvertently removed from the bottom of the eastern part. But fortunately the western part of the pond was left undisturbed and there still remain the original gravel and clay used for hardening the bottom, showing the technique used in the Heian period (ninth and tenth centuries). The rock composition as well as the plan of some of the islands, still preserve the original aspect.

27

GARDEN OF DAISHU-IN, KYOTO. This very old garden, which originally belonged to the Tokudaiji family, was completed in the Bunji era (1185–1189) and was most beautiful until about the fifteenth century. The bottom of the pond around the middle island was hardened with clay and gravel. It occupies a fine position situated just below the famous sand-and-rock garden of Ryoan-ji. One can well imagine how wonderful the scenery round about the garden must have been when people went boating on its pond. Even now one feels close to nature in its sylvan solitude.

Area about 6 acres, including a pond of almost 2½ acres.

PHOENIX HALL GARDEN OF BYODO-IN, UJI. The Chief Counsellor Michinaga built a villa in Uji in 998, and in the following year invited notables to a boating excursion in his garden. In describing an imperial visit to this garden in 1019 the *Masu Kagami* also refers to a boating picnic, and speaks of catching small fishes with nets. It mentions an arching bridge, a boat with a dragon-head prow, and the singing of insects which added to the enjoyment. The original contour of the pond which was gravel-bottomed has been well preserved.

An Amida Hall was built in the compound of the villa and installed in it was an image of Amida 16 feet high. This beautiful temple, designed to suggest a phoenix standing with wings outspread has recently been dismantled and reconstructed and will continue to reflect its beautiful form in this ancient pond, ever reminding the observer of the refined aristocratic culture of the late Heian period. Area about $2\frac{1}{4}$ acres.

2. KAMAKURA PERIOD (1184-1333) AND YOSHINO-CHO (1334-1393)

MINAMOTO-NO YORITOMO, the founder of the Kamakura regime, was a garden enthusiast. He showed an intense interest in the laying out of a garden for the Eifuku-ji monastery in Kamakura. Before the work began a great many rocks were assembled from all over the country. He commanded the priest Seigen to arrange the rocks. Some enormous ones, measuring more than ten feet in height, were used, Hatakeyama Shigetada winning praise from Yoritomo for the way he used his marvellous strength in helping with the work. Part of the work had to be done again, but by the end of 1193 it was nearing completion. The garden and the buildings looked so beautiful that the *Azuma Kagami* described them as being excelled only by the magnificence of the scenery in the nine realms of the Buddhist Paradise in the West, there being nothing on earth to be compared with them.

The love of gardens continued strong among influential persons after Yoritomo's death. Judging from descriptions left to us, we gather that the transformation from the Heian type of garden was due to the influence of Northern Sung painting.

There were a number of great garden designers in Kamakura at this time, including Sadaie the great poet and calligrapher, Gokyogoku Yoshitsune, probable author of the famous *Sakuteiki* (Book on Making Gardens), as well as Tachibana Tomoshige and the priest Seigen.

In 1205 Gokyogoku Yoshitsune was busy constructing a garden of his own at Nakamikado in Kyoto, and was anxious to finish it in time for a feast of winding waters that he had planned. He ordered Sadaie to construct a bridge over the pond in the south garden. About a month later an aged pine-tree was transplanted into his garden and in the same year a paulownia-tree was planted in the south-west corner. Three days later he went to Higashiyama, and had a cherry-tree dug up and planted in his garden. A week later he had another cherry-tree transplanted into his garden, these trees having been transported on a cart, as described in the *Meigetsuki*. This new garden was described in the *Masu Kagami* thus: 'The garden was laid out with a pond as the main feature. A bridge was built to the middle island under the direction of Sadaie. There was a hill built in front, and a waterfall at the foot of it. The rock composition in the garden was especially beautiful. When one was in the garden one had the impression of being in the heart of deep mountains thickly covered with moss. Especially conspicuous among the ancient trees was a pine tree stretching out its branches covered in dark green foliage.'

The *Meigetsuki* records Sadaie's later visit to this garden at Nakamikado and tells how deeply he was touched as he gazed on the moon rising from behind it. It was heart-breaking to see it going to pieces, the garden which he had helped to make. The water and rocks reminded him of the old days, and tears streamed down in 'thousands and tens of thousands'.

The *Azuma Kagami* mentions how the guests assembled at another garden party, which included the Shogun Sanetomo, and praised the beautiful landscape and rare rocks used in the garden. All were agreed that Kamakura, surrounded as it was by its mountains and rivers, was an excellent place to lay out a garden. One of the advantages of having mountains and rivers close by was that they made the construction of a waterfall easier.

Remains of the GARDEN OF EIFUKU-JI, KAMAKURA. Minamoto-no Yoritomo (1146–1199), founder of the Kamakura regime, planned to establish the Eifuku-ji in Kamakura after the pattern of the Nikaido of the Dai Choju-in Monastery in Mutsu Province and began work on the project in 1189.

The site chosen was excellent and the Shogun himself supervised the work. The man directly responsible for the garden was a priest, Seigen, a great genius in landscape architecture. Enormous rocks of wonderful shapes were assembled from all over the country and placed in the pond to create an atmosphere suitable to the surrounding hills. When completed in 1193, the garden was described as wonderfully beautiful, 'even as the Buddhist paradise in the west.'

In 1211 the whole monastery was reduced to ashes, though in 1242 when the Shogun Yoritsune held a verse-making party here, the garden, though much damaged, was still very beautiful. But it became neglected and forgotten and most of its area was used for kitchen gardens or paddy-fields. Finally in recent years about one-half of the site was cleared in an effort to restore the garden. Today there is hardly any evidence of a garden there . . . no pond and only a few rocks, practically everything being completely covered by a thick growth of swamp weeds. What a tragedy! Area about 2 acres.

31

The transplanting of trees was much practised in this period and it was customary to have rare flowering plants or beautiful trees brought from distant places. Boats used in boating parties in gardens often had a richly decorated prow consisting of the head of a dragon on the neck of a *geki* (heron-like large water fowl).

While Sadaie was engaged in making a garden for Prince Saionji's villa at Kitayama in Kyoto, he had a famous rock in the shape of a lion's head, named Hokkoseki drawn into the garden by seventeen oxen. The *Masu-Kagami* has the following comments on this garden: 'The garden's charming layout included the graceful form of a mountain, with deep forest, and a lake filled with water simulating the sea. The water falling from the peak thundered and the ground trembled. The profoundness that went into the making of the garden moved one to tears.'

It should be noted that the garden designers of Kamakura were generally Buddhist priests, while those of Kyoto were usually aristocrats.

As was the case during Heian times the gardens of this period were made for aristocrats and the military class. Gardens of such temples as Saiho-ji, Tenryu-ji, Nanzen-in, and Senshu-ji were originally laid out as large lake gardens for the Imperial family, noblemen or warriors and only later came to belong to temples. None of the gardens of the Saga villa, Byodo-in or Kanshin-ji kept their original layout but they were all redesigned.

The Kamakura period was an age of militarism, power being vested in the warrior class. Those of the aristocrats of Kyoto who were sympathetic with the warrior class gained power. The gardens too were developed to suit the warrior class, so that they could be best enjoyed from the house. This characterizes the gardens of this period. On the other hand, Buddhism went through many changes and reforms, with consequent changes in its influence. The development of the Zen sect of Buddhism in particular was to have a strong influence.

Thus there existed in this period the following three types: the garden planned to be viewed from the studies of members of the warrior class; the type showing the influence of the *shindenzukuri* type of architecture, and another type connected with the Zen sect.

TOJI-IN GARDEN, KYOTO. Though the older part of this garden has generally been accredited to Muso Kokushi, some scholars think he had nothing to do with it. There seems very little of the original garden left. Many trees and rocks were taken from this garden and transported to the garden of the Silver Pavilion which the Shogun Yoshimasa was making. The most dilapidated section of the garden still preserves the atmosphere of the Yoshino-cho, its present form corresponding with an old map preserved in the temple.

It has a tortoise island, symbolic of long life and happiness. Rocks indicate the head and legs as may be seen here. Area about $1\frac{1}{4}$ acres.

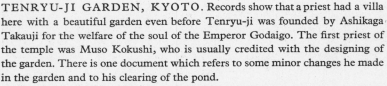

TENRYU-JI GARDEN, KYOTO. Records show that a priest had a villa here with a beautiful garden even before Tenryu-ji was founded by Ashikaga Takauji for the welfare of the soul of the Emperor Godaigo. The first priest of the temple was Muso Kokushi, who is usually credited with the designing of the garden. There is one document which refers to some minor changes he made in the garden and to his clearing of the pond.

The original garden may have been laid more than 100 years before his time, with Tachibana Tomoshige as the possible designer. This would place the garden as early as the middle of the Kamakura period, along with the Saga-in garden, of which the lake and some of the original rocks are near the Daigaku-ji Monastery, not far from Tenryu-ji.

The garden was on a higher level than the River Oigawa as it flows nearby at the foot of Arashiyama (a beauty-spot famed for its cherry-blossom) but after some difficulty water was led into it by means of a water-wheel.

Its possession of a 'dragon-pond' does not necessarily mean that the pond was dug in that shape, but that people believed that a dragon lived in it. It still retains a rock composition symbolizing a carp leaping up the cataract Lung-men, then turning into a dragon as it ascends still higher, an ancient Chinese tradition, while the stone bridge, seen here, marks the place where the water of the cascade was made to fall into the pond.

Takauji transplanted twenty white cherry-trees and crimson maples as the background for the garden. When Yoshimasa visited Tenryu-ji he praised the scenery, saying: 'With maple-trees all around the arbour, Arashiyama looked like brocade'. Area about 1 acre.

34

GARDEN OF SHOMYO-JI AT KANAZAWA, near Yokohama. The Shomyo-ji temple was established here in 1260 by Hojo Sanetoki for the welfare of his mother's soul, while the present temple bell was cast in 1269 for that of his father. The beautiful tone of the bell has long been admired as one of the eight celebrated things of Kanazawa. From his boyhood Sanetoki was very fond of learning. He collected many books, some copied or imported from China, and by 1275 the Kanazawa library was established for the purpose of benefiting those who wished to advance their learning. The library is still in existence, being now housed in a modern fireproof reinforced concrete building close to the pond in the garden.

The garden is now more the library's than the temple's but retains the peace and tranquillity which led Sanetoki to build his villa here nearly 700 years ago. Some islands remain, and some old trees are still thriving, including a plum-tree and maple-trees.

3. MUROMACHI PERIOD (1394-1572)

GARDEN-MAKING and the visiting of gardens became very fashionable in this period. In 1402 the first party from Ming China came on such a visit and others followed two years later and in the following three years. It was customary on these occasions to compose poems on the gardens visited. It should be noted that as new gardens came into existence others had to suffer by losing rocks and trees, for it became impossible to obtain garden materials by legitimate means. Also it seems to have been customary to ask for a rock or tree to complete one's garden or to exchange rocks and trees.

This custom continued into the Momoyama period which followed. Take for instance the rock named Fujito-seki now in the Sanbo-in garden. It was first in the garden of the Hosokawa mansion, but was taken to the Nijo Castle when that garden was made. From there it was removed to Hideyoshi's Juraku villa and finally brought to its present site.

The gardeners who actually made the garden were called *kawaharamono* and usually were looked down upon. However, the Shogun Yoshimasa treated two of them, Zen-ami and Matashiro, very well, and they were given an allowance for their excellent services.

The comments that one can read in diaries and poems of the period are usually restricted to remarks about whether the cherries were in bloom, or the plum had good fragrance, or the willow growing on the bank had cast pleasant green shadows on the water, but certainly the number of comments shows at least that gardens were more popular than formerly.

Yoshimasa, together with other noblemen and feudal lords of the time, enjoyed the beauty of gardens and the nature they reflected. People of the time seem to have been attracted most by the trees, especially by the flowers of the spring and crimson leaves of the autumn. On the whole they paid very little attention to the rock compositions, but there were exceptions, for when Yoshimasa visited Rokuo-in the priest of the temple reported to him that he had had all the rocks in the garden covered up with earth during the Onin Wars and found them all safely afterwards.

One of the most important aesthetic ideas in the Muromachi period was that true art had always a concealed, secret component. This secret part was called the artist's 'flower'. That which was not concealed could not be a flower for, it was said, no flower that fell still remained on the tree. So the reasoning went, but in a style which seemed to seek to conceal the truth.

The word *yugen*, originally meaning 'mystery', came to be used as synonymous with the highest attribute of art.

It was the nuance not expressed in words. It was a view that one cannot see. When the thought was deep, and words exquisite, *yugen* was there just as in the autumn evening when there was no scene, no colour, no voice to attract one's attention, nothing extraordinary at all, yet tears flowed of their own accord.

Seami said the substance of *yugen* was beautiful and soft. Shotetsu observed that *yugen* was in the heart and not in words. It was something which one cannot describe with words such as 'interesting' or 'mysterious'; it is shapeless and intangible.

Not only the drama and poetry, but also the gardens of this period had to contain the quality of *yugen*, though, as we shall see, this was not the only influence. It is no longer possible to disentangle the intermingled ideas of Horai and the Buddhist paradise. When applied to gardens, *yugen* called for hidden meaning behind the mere external layout.

At the beginning of this period, when the grounds of the Golden Pavilion were laid out, the villa garden was still lingering from the previous period and the garden that required to be viewed from a boat on the lake still persisted. But later a new type became popular that was made to be appreciated from a fixed point and it became impossible to construct a Horai type as perfect as the Golden Pavilion garden on account of the great expense and the large area required.

The white sand cone and platform which forms part of the garden of the Silver Pavilion was an early step toward the dry landscape, which was later to become independent as, for example, in Daisen-in. Notice that something of the sort had existed in the Kamakura period, for the *Sakuteiki* had mentioned 'a garden without a pond or stream called a dry landscape'. However, the following elements had entered into the art of garden-making before the complete development of the dry landscape was reached:

1. Development of gardens of the *kansho* type, planned to be ornamental and viewed from one position, brought with it a diminution in area. This was linked with the change from *shinden-zukuri* architecture to that of the warrior's house, the *shoin* (guest-room or study) of which was the point from which the garden was looked at.

2. The *kansho* style resulted in simplification and suggestion (*yugen*) in the construction of the garden. Each rock composition came to represent crane and tortoise islands, as well as Horai and waterfalls. Each stone or tree came to represent a whole landscape.

3. The influence of the black and white of Sung painting was strong. Sand represented white silk or paper, while the rock composition suggested the drawing in black. Flat painting was thus given depth and a third dimension.

Added to these was the influence of the theory of *in* and *yo* which was influential at the time. An excellent example of this is found in the Silver Pavilion garden in which one-half of the garden is occupied by a pond and the other half by a heap of sand. One is *in* and the other *yo*.

Thus, instead of being drawn with ink and brush, the picture came to be drawn on the ground with trees and rocks, a great step forward in the progress of painting and also in the development of the garden.

The building of pavilions in the garden may be looked upon as an influence of the ideas of Paradise or of Horai.

Instead of using rocks of about the same height as their breadth, as were used in the earlier periods, ones that were taller came to be employed. These rocks gave the impression that they had been artificially created and groups of them acquired great strength of emphasis.

The dry landscape was pictorial with a tendency to become cubic. What had been symbolically expressed in black ink was removed even further from reality when expressed in rocks. Thus the symbolic composition in Daisen-in suggested drawings of Ma Yüan or Hsia-Kuei, and that of Taizo-in in Myoshin-ji reproduced landscapes by Mu Ch'i. A single rock was made to represent or symbolize a mountain or falling water. Rocks became symbols of landscapes rather than things of beauty. In the case of the Daisen-in, a rock $7\frac{1}{2}$ feet high is erected together with two rocks 5 feet high. They represent high mountains in the middle distance. In Taizo-in the rock used in front, $3\frac{1}{4}$ feet high, represents a high mountain in the middle distance and a waterfall is shown at the back on the right. In the case of Daisen-in the rocks were planted almost erect, while those of Taizo-in were set slanting. In the case of Daisen-in, the rocks taper at the top, which is suggestive of the brush work of northern Sung painting, while the Taizo-in ones are suggestive of southern Sung painting.

Generally there is an artificial hill at the back of a dry waterfall, but there is none at Daisen-in, where the rock-composition itself symbolizes high mountains. The waterfall at Daisen-in is represented as having many levels, and a continuous composition of rocks is used, whereas at the Taizo-in, each rock stands separate. The former suggests the older technique that prevailed in the Kamakura and Yoshino-cho periods, while the latter shows a newer technique which continued into the Momoyama period.

With the general simplification of dry landscapes, Horai could be suggested by a single rock.

In a pond garden the rock composition which represents the crane island is set on the middle island in the pond garden; generally something like a slab is erected as a symbolic suggestion of a feather. In the case of the dry landscape, the group is not detached as an island, but treated as a part of the composition symbolizing mountains.

A similar treatment is given to the tortoise island.

The combination of 7, 5 and 3 rocks is represented in the garden of the Ryoan-ji and the Shinju-an. In the case of Ryoan-ji, they are subdivided and, counting from east, grouped in 5, 2, 3, 2 and 3. But in the Shinju-an they are grouped, counting from the south, in 7, 5 and 3.

Though the rocks at Ryoan-ji seem to have been planted deep in the ground, in reality they are not; they are known to be almost entirely on the surface.

Some 'thrown-away' rocks (*sute-ishi*) are used in the Daisen-in. These too should be regarded as being due to the influence of painting.

In the pond type garden water was often made to run down the rock composition representing a cataract in the Muromachi period, though there are some exceptions. But in the Momoyama and subsequent periods they often had a dry waterfall.

Rock islands symbolizing nine mountains and eight seas, based on ancient Hindu cosmology, are also found in some gardens of this period. In short, the dry landscape had already appeared in the Nara period as a part of the garden. It gradually developed through the Kamakura period and matured by the middle of Muromachi period when the black and white drawings of the northern and southern Sung period began to influence our gardens. Dry landscape gardens of the independent type came to appear after the middle of the Muromachi period. They were created as a kind of painting, and a rock was used as a mountain, a waterfall, a stream or a boat. Thus in the dry landscape garden a rock was no longer mere material for constructing a garden, but resembled a mountain, or waterfall or other objects in pictorial art.

The whole garden became as a painting, but not merely a reproduction of a painting. It became an original work rich in creative quality. A composition of rocks in this new art form contributed not only a beautiful effect but added also a symbolic expression.

This applies to the stone garden of Ryoan-ji. It needs no background, being enclosed by walls, entirely detached from the rest of the world.

Dry landscapes, especially a garden like that of the Ryoan-ji, should be considered in connection with *bonseki*, which developed in the Muromachi period and has a great number of followers in Japan. *Bonseki* is a branch of art depicting landscapes with small stones and sand on black-lacquered trays, used as decoration in the house.

KAMEISHI-BO GARDEN, MOUNT HIKOSAN, FUKUOKA. The great painter Sesshu spent some time in Kyushu after his return from Ming China and before designing the garden for Joei-ji in Yamaguchi. During his stay he designed this garden, high up on a slope of Mount Hiko in Kyushu. The temple is no longer in existence, but the garden is still in a fairly good condition, and covered with the moss of ages. It occupies a commanding spot, and has a pond which is fed by a spring further up on the wooded slope. This is sylvan solitude in the bosom of nature, a fit place for meditation.

39

KINKAKU-JI (GOLDEN PAVILION) GARDEN, KYOTO. During his lifetime, Yoshimitsu (3rd Ashikaga Shogun) ordered his villa to be turned into a temple, and it was named Rokuon-ji, meaning the Temple of the Deer Park, where Buddha first preached after attaining enlightenment. The intention apparently was to symbolize a Buddhist paradise in the garden, though the gardeners freely introduced tortoise and crane islands, emblems of a long life and happiness of the Horai landscape. These separate ideals are harmoniously commingled. Some of the stone compositions are interpreted as signifying Shumisen.

The temple is also known as Kinkaku-ji (Golden Pavilion) symbolizing the palace of dragons under the sea, so graphically suggested by the beautiful building reflected in the mirror of the lake. Furthermore, in the original plan when the lake was much larger, the pavilion may have stood in the water.

This garden is generally attributed to Soami, but he does not appear in documents as having done anything as a gardener. One named Kyuei, however, had a great deal to do with it, according to the diary relating to its construction.

The upper picture shows a rock combination for a spring which was used by Yoshimitsu to obtain water for his *cha no yu*.

The Golden Pavilion was destroyed by fire a few years ago, and a new building is now being built after the original plan. One illustration shows it as it looks today, and others how it looked before the fire (and how it will appear when it is completed). In front of that building are two small tortoise and crane islands, with many smaller islands, some representing tortoises swimming to and fro.

Area about 4½ acres including the pond of 1¾ acres.

GARDEN OF JOEI-JI (also called Sesshu-ji), YAMAGUCHI. Sesshu (1420–1509) was contemporary with Zen-ami and Matashiro. Though geniuses, as gardeners they were looked down upon as persons of low vocation. But Sesshu was a great painter and created in his gardens great nature, as he created it in his paintings.

During the twenty years after his return from Ming China in 1470 he made many gardens, among them the Joei-ji garden for Ouchi Masahiro who was in power at that time. Ouchi wanted his garden to look like that of the Kinkaku-ji. It has been much praised and a poem on the garden says: 'The design is full of unexpected turns. Groups of three mountains and five peaks are surrounded by mysterious seas. The composition of rocks even now seems like dragons and tigers at war. The boundless water extends to heaven and one feels oneself in the precincts of Horai'.

It still retains its essential features: a pond and *kare-sansui* (dry landscape) of a sauntering type, and a rock composition on the hillside with a gorgeous cataract, the water being made to fall in seven levels. It shows Sesshu's intimate knowledge of the natural scenery of China, and reflects the gardens of the Northern Sung dynasty, particularly in its three-dimensional planning. Neither did he ignore the Japanese rules for garden-making. Since this was made for Ouchi's samurai-style *shoin* the garden suggested a Horai landscape containing crane and tortoise islands. In the dry landscape, Sesshu used for the principal rock one with a flat top, combined with others in slanting positions. Beautiful lines of composition were aimed at, and all the rocks showed rhythmic movements. The result was superb. Each composition was related to other groups. A group of three was related to a group of two, another group of two related to still another of two etc. Each stone by its inclination expresses some power: one inclined to the right and the other to the left: one stands, the other sits or lies down, one high, the other low.

There is profound tranquillity among the rocks and a clear gushing spring. Area about 7 acres.

GARDEN OF JOEI-JI, (also called Sesshu-ji) YAMAGUCHI

DAIJO-IN GARDEN SITE, NARA. In 1451 fire destroyed all the buildings of Daijo-in but the work of the restoration of its garden was begun soon after, for it is recorded that one white *maki* (*podocarpus chinensis*) and a five-needle pine were transplanted thither in 1459, and another five-needle pine from Taian-ji and a plum-tree from Gokurakubo in the same year.

According to the *Shinsen Tokyo Meisho Zue* written in the Keian era (1649–1651) Kanamori Sowa, a famous tea master of the time, was commissioned to construct a *chaseki* called *rokusoan* (six-window hut) in the garden of the Jigan-in, a tributary temple of the Kofuku-ji. This seems to have been removed to the garden of the Daijo-in some time later and now stands in the rear garden of Tokyo National Museum.

The garden was devastated in 1887. But three old drawings have been preserved, and from these we know that what now remains of the once glorious garden of Daijo-in maintains the original plan more or less intact: there are five small islands, one of which is reached by a bridge. Area about 2¾ acres.

DAIJO-IN GARDEN SITE, NARA

44

DAISEN-IN GARDEN, KYOTO. Daisen-in was completed in 1512 or 1513. It is a dry landscape of the *Horai* type, typical not only of a Zen temple garden, but also of that of the warrior's study.

The following incident is said to be illustrated in this garden: 'Buddha held up a flower and Kasyapa smiled'. This is regarded as the beginning of the tradition on which Zen Buddhism based its existence. Buddha saw that he alone among his disciples understood what he meant. What it was he understood is not to be explained in words.

The garden looks very simple, but it is complex in its content. Even great scholars have been unable to grasp its real beauty. However, viewed in one light, the symbolic content dissolves into a bit of natural scenery in a ravine—with a waterfall suggested by rocks among mountains, symbolized by clipped shrubs; there are also streams with a dam, a boat and other things symbolically expressed.

This is a superb example of gardening art. Area about 120 square yards.

RYOAN-JI GARDEN, KYOTO. A rectangular piece of ground with fifteen rocks, the intervening spaces being filled with white sand, which is raked in different patterns. No tree is growing in the garden.

Ryoan-ji garden seems to have been restored after a fire in 1488 and was endowed by Tokugawa Iyeyasu and Iyemitsu. It was again damaged by fire in 1797. Various names have been offered as possible designers of the garden, but no one has prevailed. Some scholars assert that the two names carved on one of the stones in the garden—Kotaro and Hikojiro—are probably those of the men who made this unique and famous garden. It is generally taken to show a strong influence of the black-and-white paintings of the Sung and Yüan dynasties. It is however more than merely pictorial; it is symbolic, but the interpretation of its symbol depends upon the individual. Area about 360 square yards.

46

GINKAKU-JI (Silver Pavilion) GARDEN, KYOTO. As soon as one enters the garden, one is struck by its beauty and tranquillity. One is also impressed by the excellent state of preservation of the original features, such as the rock compositions, due to the care taken of the garden through the centuries.

The slope of the hill overlooking the garden was excavated some 24 years ago, and many of the rocks were found to be in their original places. The dry landscape higher upon the hillside makes the layout similar to that of the Saiho-ji garden (frontispiece).

Here are views of the garden and the islands from the upper floor of the silver pavilion. The garden is mainly a *kaiyu-shiki* type, though not exclusively so. It has, as shown here, a pile of white sand in the form of a truncated cone about 6 feet high, the diameter at the base being about 16 feet and at the top, 5 feet, and a platform built of white sand just over 2 feet high, the white sand covering being about 7 inches thick. No one is certain about the real purpose of the sand piles, which are peculiar to this garden. But we are told that when viewed from the upper floor of the pavilion in the moonlight, the truncated cone appears like a silvery full moon reflected on the earth and the platform gives the appearance of a silver lake. Area about 1¾ acres.

4. MOMOYAMA PERIOD (1573-1602)

THE custom of making presents of trees and rocks to a friend for his garden continued into this period. It seemed customary for the recipient of the presents to send vehicles and men to transport the gifts to his garden.

As in the previous period, gardens still being a great attraction, many new ones were created and many writings purporting to contain secrets discovered by great gardeners were circulated among their followers. One of the diaries mentions the washing of the pine-tree in the football ground. It seems that usually the following four trees were planted one at each corner of the square: pine, willow, cherry and maple, and that these trees had to be washed from time to time.

When Nobunaga constructed a garden for the Nijo Palace he commandeered rocks from various temples and from mansions or belonging to feudal lords. But soon after the garden was finished he had most of its rocks and trees transported to Azuchi where he began building another residence. Influential people of the time seem to have derived great joy in laying out a new garden, but to have thought nothing of tearing down an existing one.

One of the diaries mentions a gardener named Yasokuro, an expert in clipping hedges of which a great deal was made in the early Momoyama period. The same diary mentions a plum-blossom-viewing party on the 17th day of the 2nd month of 1579. It had been customary from Heian times to hold such a party on moonlight nights as on this occasion. The thought of using the garden at night as well as in the day must have been kept in mind by the gardeners as one can deduce from the amazement of the effect of moonlight on white sand in the Silver Pavilion Garden, Kyoto.

The garden made for Nobunaga's castle at Azuchi on the banks of Lake Biwa astonished the warriors who gathered there when it was completed. Wonderful rocks and rare trees were assembled not only from the new garden of the Nijo castle, but also from various other gardens and famous places in the neighbourhood. Even some *sotetsu* palms (*Cycas revoluta*) were transplanted from Myokoku-ji in Sakai.

It may be well for us to remember that during this period Hideyoshi had built his castle at Fushimi for the erection of which more than 200,000 men were used. The project included the garden of the keep, later reconstructed in the Honganji temple, and another for the mansion occupied by Hideyoshi's wife: this was later reconstructed to be her brother's home, near the Kodai-ji temple.

As was the case in the Muromachi period, those who made the gardens during this period, such as Sen, the Yoshiro brothers, Asagiri Shimanosuke and Kentei, were looked down upon.

Peculiarities in the rock composition representing Shumisen are shown in this period. It was mainly based on the symbolic expression of Buddhist doctrines. For that reason several stones were arranged in a circle and a rock was erected in the centre. During this period comparatively small stones had been used in the circle, all placed flat, and the height of the central rock varied. In some instances there was a tall rock, more than five feet high, but many of those which were erected late in the period were low and gave an impression of weakness.

During this period a new type of garden was developed, the *Roji* or garden-path to the *chaseki* or tea room. The *Roji* and *chaseki* developed swiftly as the tea ceremony came to assume greater importance, and contributed much towards the development of the garden as a whole, fostering the spirit of simplicity, in harmony with the newly-introduced stepping stones and stone lanterns hitherto used in the shrines and temples. There were also introduced *tsukubai* or stone water-basins for the purpose of purification. Though actually very small, and not more than a path, some *Roji* gave the feeling of mystic profundity and tranquillity.

There were the following garden styles prevalent in this period: (a) that which followed the dry landscape style of the Muromachi period, (b) that which sought to develop the Horai type along the line of water gardens, (c) another group which tried to harmonize these two groups, and (d) still another group which turned its attention to the development of *Roji* or *chaseki* gardens. Since the Momoyama period was a sort of revival, even those who clung to the old ideals of the Muromachi period, and abided by the dry landscape style, could not help being influenced by the new movements. This was especially marked in the treatment of materials, such as small stones for paving to suggest the flow of a stream.

In other respects as well, the tendency was to turn away from the pictorial effect and towards naturalistic expression.

KOJO-IN GARDEN. OTSU, SHIGA PREFECTURE. According to a tradition of the temple, this garden was laid out by Yamaoka Doami in 1601. But the garden may be older, perhaps dating from the end of Muromachi or early Momoyama. The present building was evidently built when there already existed a garden, as part of it is over the rocks and pond.

The plan of the garden is that of a Horai landscape with a row of rocks representing ships anchored at night. There is a tortoise island connected to the mainland by a stone bridge, but no crane island. Mainly because of the closeness of the building to the base of a steep hill, the garden was made to be best enjoyed from the *shoin*.

Both mountain and river rocks of dark colour are used. The clear water of the pond, in keeping with these rocks and the moss-covered hillside, gives one a feeling of freshness and profound tranquillity. Area about $\frac{1}{10}$ acre.

49

GARDEN OF THE NISHI HONGAN-JI AUDIENCE CHAMBER, KYOTO. According to a temple tradition, it was in 1632 that the Hongan-ji temple received as a gift from Tokugawa Iyemitsu the audience hall, *no* stage and other buildings from Hideyoshi's residence, the Fushimi Palace. When these buildings were removed and reconstructed on the present site as parts of the temple, stones and plants belonging to the audience chamber in the Fushimi Castle were brought here by Asagiri Shimano-suke. The garden is believed to have been originally laid out in the castle during the three years beginning in 1592. There is a very close resemblance between it and that of the Sanbo-in, though this is a flat and dry landscape and the other had actual waterfalls and ponds.

There is an arched stone bridge from the crane to the tortoise island. It must have been perfectly in keeping with the Fushimi Castle. How superb it looks and how it reminds us of the personality of Hide-yoshi for whom it was made! How symbolic it is of the bold spirit of the Momoyama period!

The garden is so laid out as to be best appreciated from the chamber in which Hideyoshi used to give audiences to his feudal lords. It is known as *Kokei no niwa* (garden of the tiger-valley) for it depicts a famous landscape of that name in China, which has been a favourite subject for gardens since the Muromachi period. Thus the garden is an astonishingly harmonious combination of apparently incongruous elements. Area about ¼ acre.

GARDEN IN NAGOYA CASTLE. Records show that these gardens in the Nagoya Castle were constructed and re-modelled during the Tenbun (1532–1545), the Koji (1555–1557), the Bunroku (1592–1594) and the Keicho (1596–1614) eras.

The stone composition symbolizes the Horai crane and tortoise. Water was used to a limited extent, but the greater portion was in dry landscape. *Sotetsu* or sago palms (*Cyeas revoluta*) which were fashionable in the Momoyama and Early Edo periods, are effectively used. The enormous rocks used in the composition seem to reveal the powerful spirit of the age, giving an impression of that emphasis upon strength and power that the generals of the time craved after. Only great masters are able to bring out the hidden qualities of such rocks.

51

NIJO PALACE GARDEN, KYOTO. It seems that the present garden of the Nijo Palace was complete when Iyeyasu came to occupy it in 1601. Records show that the garden was remodelled in 1624 under the direction of Kobori Enshu.

On the whole the garden is of the Horai type, with crane and tortoise islands. It is known as the garden of *Ni-no maru* (second keep) of the Nijo Palace and it has also been known as *Hachijin-no Niwa* (garden of 8 camps), the arrangement and grouping of rocks being based on strategic principles, with 7 camps surrounding the general's headquarters in the centre. Its pond covers about ⅖ acre and has a flat bottom paved with small stones (the waterfall at the north-west corner can be seen): water can be led from the river Horikawa, but the pond is generally kept dry. The grouping of the rocks and their vertical setting show the influence of the Muromachi period. There is a feeling of magnificence in keeping with the palace.

KONCHI-IN GARDEN, KYOTO. Enshu is believed to have designed and supervised the work on this garden, though no mention of this is made in authentic records, and the date when the work was begun or completed is not precisely known. The garden is of the crane-tortoise type, and the technique used and the plan followed induce us to believe that Enshu had a hand in it.

This garden is a very characteristic dry landscape with *Horai* elements. The south garden of the main temple is largely covered with white sand in the general shape of a boat. It represents or symbolizes a boat in relation to the island of Horai. At the same time the sand represents a great ocean.

These rock compositions symbolizing *horai-zan* are worthy of study. The interrelation between the lines of one rock and those of the others, creates a wonderful feeling of rhythm. Not only that, but the different angles they form, some acute and others obtuse, show very careful study. Balance and proportion, are essential aesthetic elements in the Far East. Area about 1½ acres.

JUKO-IN GARDEN, Tributary Temple of DAITOKU-JI. This garden has been attributed to Rikyu, but some scholars are inclined to believe that it was laid out earlier, perhaps about the Eiroku era (1558–1569) when the Superior's quarters in the temple were constructed. It is of the Shumisen type and suitable to the Zen temple. The pictorial construction of the dry garden, which was emphasized in the Muromachi period, was no longer completely kept up here. But the desire to evoke a mysterious and profound atmosphere in a garden was still strong. This end was sought through a somewhat crude form of beauty.

54

JISSO-AN ROJI, SAKAI. There are a number of gardens in Sakai which are attributed to Rikyu, and this *roji* is also accredited to him. That was quite natural, for Rikyu was born here, and his old home and *chaseki* still exist here.

When the Jisso-an *chaseki* (now at the Manshu-ji) was at the Entetsu-ji Temple in another part of the city, Rikyu is said to have planted the hedge in front of the *chaseki*, shutting off the view of the sea, and allowing a glimpse of it only when at the water-basin.

GYOKUHO-IN GARDEN, MYOSHIN-JI, KYOTO. It is evident that the present temple was rebuilt in 1656 and though no exact date is to be found for the layout of the garden, it is believed that it was already in existence in 1560.

The garden is a dry landscape built for a residence containing a Shumisen composed of huge rocks in the manner of the early Momoyama period. The use of sago palm came into fashion at this time. Though greatly damaged, the garden still bears traces, such as the stone lantern, of the grandeur of former days. The Horai idea is strong, making it more suitable for a dwelling than for a Zen temple.

56

MYOKI-AN ROJI, YAMAZAKI. According to the illustrations in the *Sanshu Meiseki-shi*, there was a large tree named *Sode suri matsu* (sleeve-brushing pine-tree) growing in the garden close to the tea room which was built in 1606. But a little later a publication comments that the sleeve-brushing pine was then gone: 'in the same spot now grows a pine-tree about 9 feet in circumference'. This is believed to be a second pine planted in the same spot some 200 years ago.

The garden has two stone water-basins said to date from the time when Hideyoshi drank tea in the two-mat tea room, at a time when his forces were engaged in a battle against Mitsuhide.

SANBO-IN GARDEN, SUBURB OF KYOTO. Hideyoshi paid a visit to the Sanbo-in early in 1598 and decided upon a plan for remodelling the garden. This consisted of making a middle island, connecting it with the mainland by a bridge, and constructing two waterfalls. In the course of the work a change was made in the plan and a peninsula was substituted for the middle island. Hideyoshi had wanted this garden completed in time to hold a cherry-blossom viewing party on the 15th day of the 3rd month of that year, but that was impossible. On the 8th of the 4th month a gardener Sen brought with him about 300 labourers and on the following day the celebrated rock named *Fujito-seki* was moved from Juraku (Hideyoshi's villa in Kyoto) to this garden. On the 27th day plants and moss were brought in. On the 3rd of the 5th month materials for stone bridges arrived and on the 7th waterfalls started to flow and the completion of the garden was reported to Hideyoshi.

The first stage of the work done on this garden took only forty days, but it took some twenty years to complete. More than 700 rocks were assembled, and several thousand plants were brought in from various places.

The garden has ponds and is of the sauntering type. It has Horai elements, with crane and tortoise islands, and, in addition, there is natural scenery, with waterfalls to the east and hills to the south. The intimate relationship between the garden and the building can be seen.

Altogether there were built in this garden three earthen, one wooden, and five stone bridges in order to get variety of scenes. The main waterfall was arranged in three levels, all evenly spaced and water was led into side avenues, as it were, to create a change of atmosphere. This has given dignity and refinement to the garden.

Area about $1\frac{1}{3}$ acres.

5. EARLY EDO PERIOD (1603-1680)

AFTER political power had fallen into the hands of the Tokugawa Shogun, the gardens belonging to feudal lords closely connected with the Tokugawa, as well as temples and shrines related in some manner to the reigning power, were the first to receive attention.

In some cases new gardens were laid out, in others the existing gardens were expanded or remodelled. Generally speaking the trend of the gardens of the Momoyama period continued, but with less vigour and magnificence.

Yet there was a striking development in the *chaseki* gardens, which featured simplicity and refined poverty. With the rapid progress of the tea ceremony accelerated by the appearance of tea-masters of great originality, there was a revolution in the gardens of Japan.

A movement was started to revive the dry landscape gardens of the Muromachi period, and flat gardens were started for the *shoin* of Zen temples. The traditional form of rock compositions for Shumisen and Horai was abandoned, and people began making gardens, unfettered by any established rules and traditions. Gardens were no longer confined to a special class of people and became popularized.

Many books were written, setting forth the fundamentals for planning a garden, such as utilizing the natural contour of the land reproducing some famous scenery.

The types or styles of this period may be roughly grouped as follows :

1. *Kaiyu-shiki* with paths around the pond to saunter along to enjoy the garden from every angle.

2. *Chisen Kansho-shiki*. A garden with a pond to be enjoyed from a given point in the building.

3. *Kare Sansui* (dry landscape). A cataract was constructed with rocks but no actual water was used.

4. *Roji* (path garden). There were two types, a simple form connected with a *chaseki* modelled on a hermitage, and a combination of hermitage *roji* and *shoin* garden.

From another viewpoint, these gardens, except for the *roji* may be said to be mainly of the Horai style, and attached to residences of the military class. This style generally has crane and tortoise islands in the garden pond, though sometimes only a tortoise island. In the latter case the stone composition representing the crane was included in that of the cataract.

Constructed also in this period were *Shakkei* type of gardens, as well as the *Shukkei* type. The former were gardens which 'borrowed' natural scenes or objects from outside, and thus appeared larger than they actually were. The latter was the type which reproduced a scene reduced in scale.

In the beginning of this period the rock composition for the cataract was practically the same as that in Momoyama times, a peculiarity being that three rocks might be placed at the top to represent a Buddhist Trinity. Another point of difference was the use of slabs for the water to fall upon, and that all the water might be made to fall from one level.

Instead of placing one or two slabs to represent the feather of the crane, a large rock slightly tilted outward came to be used. In the case of the tortoise the stones for the legs were often omitted on the side not seen.

60

DENPO-IN GARDEN, ASAKUSA, TOKYO. Situated at Asakusa, the Coney Island of Tokyo, Denpo-in is one of the most popular temples in this city, especially for its Buddhist deity Kwannon (Goddess of Mercy) whose tiny image is said to have been drawn up from sea in a fisherman's net as long ago as 628. The present garden is generally attributed to Kobori Enshu. It shows the influence of secular gardens by joining two ponds of different elevations by means of a stream, over which is a bridge. This makes it possible to view its central feature from one given point in the house. A group of rocks at a higher elevation composed as a dry bed of a cataract, seems the oldest part, and it shows a formula of rock composition which was prevalent in the Momoyama period. Area nearly 3 acres.

Many feudal lords of the time constructed castles in their domains and a number of gardens were laid out for the enjoyment of themselves and their families, as well as for their retinue. Most of them, if not all, tried to live up to the ideal that good feudal lords should take their pleasure after their people had had theirs, and that they should worry before their people began to worry. Some of the gardens were named to express that ideal, such as Koraku-en (after-pleasure) or Kairaku-en (pleasure shared with their people).

It was quite natural for these feudal lords to wish for prosperity and happiness for themselves and their descendants. For that reason most of the gardens included a symbolic representation of Horai together with crane and tortoise islands. In this type of garden the auspicious elements were naturally essential, though care was taken not to mar the aesthetic beauty of the garden.

Sand had been utilized as a material in the Muromachi period but it was in the Early Edo that it became an effective medium for beautiful designs, but in spite of everything there was a strong tendency in this period for the garden to grow more and more realistic and naturalistic. For this reason streams began to play an important part in the garden, it being more natural for the water to flow into the pond through a stream than to pour abruptly into it from a waterfall.

A typical garden plan for the home of feudal lords of the Edo period.

SHUGAKU-IN: UPPER GARDEN OF THE IMPERIAL PALACE, KYOTO.

Shugaku-in consists of the upper, the middle and the lower gardens with tea-houses, occupying in all about 6½ acres, in addition to nearly 40 acres of background forest. Gomizunoo Tenno, who was a poet and excelled in arranging flowers, spent much of his time designing gardens when he had abdicated in 1630 after 19 years' reign. He designed Sento Gosho Palace garden and also the Shugaku-in gardens.

This garden is situated at the base of the mountain, and utilizes the superb scenery which it commands. The greatest feature of the Upper Garden is the wonderful slope of hills covered with neatly clipped shrubbery of various species. It gives exquisitely variegated colouring, changing according to the seasons.

SHUGAKU-IN: MIDDLE GARDEN. One of the photographs shows a flight of stone steps leading up to the *Shinden zukuri* architecture of the Middle Garden. The Upper Garden adheres more or less to the type suitable to *chaseki*, with paths leading now to places of tranquillity, now to an open view across the valley extending to the further range of hills. This Middle Garden is on the southern side of the residence and is so laid as to be mainly enjoyed from the guest room. A little waterfall feeds the stream flowing in front of the *shoin*.

64

SHUGAKU-IN: LOWER GARDEN. The path strewn with white sand and edged with clipped bushes and low stone lanterns of varying designs, help to create a charming impression of sylvan solitude. From the small wooden buildings which each garden contains one can enjoy a view or privacy as desired. Going through these gardens of Shugaku-in one will notice the sparing use of rocks, though there are some in group compositions. This may be considered as a feature of the *shoin* style path-garden in which profundity and tranquillity are aimed at.

Left: The general layout of the three gardens of the imperial Palace, Kyoto.

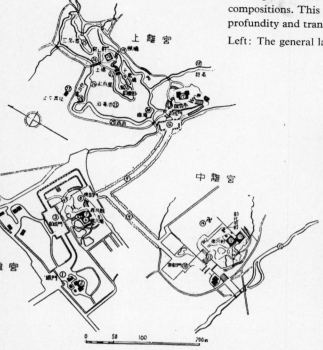

65

KOHO-AN GARDEN, KYOTO

NINNA-JI GARDEN, KYOTO. The temple of Ninnaji was established by the Emperor Koko in 885 and it is recorded that in 1890 a large number of maple-trees, and some rocks too were brought from Togano-o under the direction of a gardener named Shirai Dosho. Advantage was taken of the hill to lay the garden out in two levels. It has three *chaseki*, one of which is named *Hitotei* (flying waves arbour). Pines and maples drooped down to the water of the pond, and whenever a strong wind blew, they splashed in the water creating a scene much enjoyed from this *chaseki*, hence its name. The stone bridge leads to it.

It has well laid out paths and the garden may be appreciated as one moves about in the garden, but better still quietly from the study. It shows a transition from the *kaiyu* style toward the *kansho* style developed at the end of this period. Area about ¾ acre.

OPPOSITE: KOHO-AN GARDEN, KYOTO. This is known as the Garden of Eight Views of Omi or of the Eight Views of Hsieng-Shang. It was designed by Kobori Enshu, feudal lord of Matsuyama Castle, and was reconstructed under the direction of Fumaiko after the temple was destroyed by a fire in 1793. The house was so built as to give the occupants the feeling of being on board a boat from which they could look out upon the eight celebrated places symbolized in the garden. The name by which the *chaseki* is called reminds us of the aphorism 'Getting the thought, he forgets the word; understanding the reason, he forgets the teaching.' One of the places where one may wash one's hands before entering into the *chaseki* is seen: it must be remembered that the washing of the hands is merely a symbolic gesture of cleansing oneself spiritually as well.

As often in the Early Edo period various styles are here shown merged into a harmonious whole. The garden is planned to be viewed from the owner's study or by walking about. Area about ⅙ acre.

KIYOMIZU JOJU-IN GARDEN, KYOTO. There seems to have existed here an old garden which was badly damaged and had to be refashioned into its present form in the Early Edo period. This Joju-in Garden is one of three of the same name in Kyoto, all famous for *Setsu-getsu-ka* (snow, moon and flowers) scenery. One was the Joju-in Garden of the Kitano Shrine: this was at its best in spring, with the plum-blossom of the Tenjin Shrine as its background. The second belonged to Myoman-ji in Teramachi; with the snow-covered mountain, Hieizan, as a background and was at its best in winter. This is the third, its best being late summer, with the moon rising from behind the range of Higashi-yama. The style is primarily for sauntering but with a strong inclination for appreciation from the *shoin*. In the centre of the tortoise isle there was placed as the principal rock a big stone called *Eboshi-iwa*, being so named on account of its resemblance to the *eboshi* or court head-dress. For some reason this rock has been removed to the rear.

Close to the verandah is placed the famous water-basin, the name *Tagasode* (Whose sleeve?) being derived from its resemblance to a waving long sleeve of a young girl. There are also such celebrated stone lanterns as 'Dragonfly Lantern', 'Handball Lantern' and 'Triangular Lantern'. Area about ⅛ acre.

68

ROJI OF THE SEKKA-TEI IN KINKAKU-JI, KYOTO. This pathway, as well as the *chaseki* to which it leads, was first laid out by Sowa, a great tea master, who died in 1656. The *chaseki* was destroyed by fire and reconstructed in 1874 to the original design. The *roji* consists of stepping stones, and foundation stones, mixed with long blocks of stone arranged raftwise. The bamboo fence, of a type peculiar to this temple, is known as *Kinkakuji gaki*.

SHOSEI-EN GARDEN. This is known also as Kikoku-tei. The site is generally believed to have been that of the villa of Minamoto-no-Tooru. But the old garden fell into neglect and was remodelled in this period by Ishikawa Jozan, commissioned by Priest Sennyo Shonin. It is now used as the villa of Higashi Hongan-ji. Though it has houses on three sides, and is adjacent to a busy thoroughfare with tram-cars, it still maintains the solitude of ages, with thickly wooded hills and a spacious lake with islands.

Area about 8½ acres.

ENMAN-IN GARDEN, OTSU. Enman-in, a tributary temple of Onjo-ji, was established early in the Heian period. But the present garden is believed to have been laid out immediately after the reconstruction of the living quarters of this temple in 1647. It was laid out as the *kansho* style of garden, to be appreciated from the house. Unlike many other gardens made in this period, it does not use *shakkei* or borrowed landscapes. It retains many old rocks as they were originally composed in the seventeenth century on the hillside as well as on islands in the pond at the base.

71

SENTO GOSHO GARDEN, KYO

SENTO GOSHO GARDEN, KYOTO. Sento Gosho was the residence of the abdicated Emperors. It was first established by Nobunaga in 1589, but had no garden then. Only after the buildings had been rebuilt more than once was Kobori Enshu commissioned in 1634 to see to the layout of the garden. His work can still be seen not only in the plan but in the details also. Though various changes must have been made since, every time the buildings were destroyed by fire the garden may still be looked upon as typical of the Early Edo period. It is a large *shoin* type garden, to be appreciated by boating through the ponds.

It consists of three parts which are now interpreted as *shin*, *gyo* and *so*, these terms implying decreasing degrees of formality, though such an idea may not have entered into the plan of the garden. The *shin*, or south section (extreme left), is formal and powerful with large rocks. The *gyo*, or middle section, with a waterfall, is separated from the formal part by a zigzag stone bridge with a wisteria arbour and the *so*, at the northern end, with a simpler outline, is informal.

In 1747 Reizen Tamemura, at the command of Sakuramachi Tenno, selected ten beautiful spots in this garden and gave each a name. These are known as *Sen-tei Jikkei* (ten scenes in an unworldly garden): one place is best for appreciating spring flowers and another for crimson maple leaves; one for enjoying the sound of rain on reeds, and another for the appreciation of the moon; yet another for the beauty of the reflection of the evening glow on the pond, and another for a snow scene etc.

There are now two *chaseki*, with a small garden of *yugen* type attached to each. A farm on the north, included in the garden, was intended for the education of noblemen's children in the life of the common people. In the *shin* section of the garden the sloping beach is covered with rounded stones, each of which was sent from Odawara wrapped in cotton in exchange for one measure of rice. Rock composition on the tortoise island of the *shin*, below, still shows the work of the Early Edo period.

Area about 18 acres, including 2¼ acres of ponds.

OPPOSITE: CHION-IN GARDEN, KYOTO. A fire broke out in the *hojo* of Chion-in in 1633 and consumed nearly all the buildings. But six years later the reconstruction of the buildings was completed and at about the same time the gardens seem to have been laid out under the supervision of Katakiri Sekishu.

The garden is varied in details, imparting different feelings to the observer. Here a very clever use of big rocks with stepping stones may be appreciated. It is so made as to be enjoyed from the *hojo* and is a Horai type, with crane and tortoise islands, which are now badly in disorder. But the pond, which is well-shaded by a thick growth of trees on the hillside at the back, has a feeling of mystery which is reinforced by the large rocks used with it. Area ¾ acre.

SHISENDO GARDEN, KYOTO. In the battle of Osaka Castle, Ishikawa Jozan, who designed the present garden, was wounded by an enemy's spear, but at the gate of the castle he beheaded the enemy leader. His exploit went unrewarded on the grounds that he had advanced without awaiting the order. He was still only 33, but he retired in order to care for his aged mother. This garden was made by him during the period from 1635 when he settled here until he died in 1672 at the age of 90. After his death the garden was sadly neglected and underwent drastic changes.

As might be expected from the style of his poetry, Jozan was a great admirer of China. In planning his garden he applied ideas taken from Chinese painting. He made a waterfall, guided a stream through azalea bushes and placed a stone pagoda and a rock which must have reminded him of the *Taikoseki* (great lake stone) of China. He made hedges low enough to afford him a glimpse in the middle distance of a bamboo grove and to take in a far-off view of a range of mountains. In this flat garden of white sand, fringed by the clipped azalea bushes is a single red pine. Area about ¼ acre.

SOUTH GARDEN OF DAITOKU-JI HOJO, KYOTO. The *hojo* of Daitoku-ji has two gardens: one on the south and the other on the east side, both being dry landscapes. More than three-fifths of the area of the south garden is covered with sand giving the effect of a great expanse of water. To the right is seen the gate for the Imperial messenger on a formal visit to the temple. It takes in a view of the Hieizan mountain in the far distance and the avenue of trees along the Kamo River in the middle distance.

Area about ⅛ acre.

EAST GARDEN OF DAITOKU-JI HOJO, KYOTO. There is nothing to separate the long garden on the east side of the *hojo* from the broader one on the south but they are different, and must have been designed by two different artists. The temple tradition has it that the south garden was designed by the priest Takuan (1573–1645), while the eastern one was laid out by Enshu, and this is generally believed to be not far from the truth. The clever use of clipped bushes with the stones, and also the use of double hedges are to be noted. Though now large trees outside the hedge have completely obstructed the view, originally this garden must have borrowed from the distant scenery to expand scenes suggested in its narrow strip of land. Even without the distant views, the garden holds much that is common to the spirit of the tea ceremony and to Zen profundity.

KYOTO PALACE GARDEN. The present garden seems to be the result of remodelling an older garden in the Kansei era (1789–1800), when an attempt was made to restore the Imperial palace as it was at the time of its foundation. But on the whole it maintains the style of the Early Edo period, showing a great similarity to the Sento Gosho garden which was constructed under the supervision of Enshu.

The vast space between the palace building and the garden is covered with white sand, and then the bank of the pond slopes down gradually to the water. This bank is of gravel with a few stepping-stones leading down to a large flat stone at the brink of the water. Here one feels uplifted by the solemn atmosphere, which is deepened as one goes over the bridge to the wooded opposite shore.

78

While living in his apartment here the Emperor Komei (1846–66) directed that a part of the building should be roofed with shingles so that he might appreciate the sound of the rain falling upon it. Some people like to plant broad-leafed plants, such as bananas or large-leafed oaks, close to the house so as to enjoy hearing the sound of the rain falling on them.

By entering through the inner gate one comes upon a series of enchantments such as those above.

By proceeding still further, there is a *chaseki*, and close by it a dry landscape garden, giving an unexpected surprise (below). There are a great variety of bridges: some in wood and others of stone; some simple and others quite elaborate.

RAKU-RAKU-EN, SHIGA PREFECTURE. Shiga has many outstanding gardens. This must be due to the abundance of rock material in the area, and also to the Tendai sect of Buddhism and to the taste of the *daimyos* who came there to rule. This garden was probably made about 1628, but it has been remodelled many times since then, without losing its special features. It follows the Horai plan and there are some indications that it originally had some water, though it is now dry. Area slightly less than 1 acre.

NANZEN-JI HOJO GARDEN, KYOTO. Known also as the garden of the tiger carrying its cubs across the water (*Tora no Ko Watashi*), from the supposed meaning of the rock composition, this has been attributed to Kobori Enshu. It is a dry landscape, such as was very popular at the time for Zen temples.

It looks its best from the verandah of the main temple building. The spacious foreground of the white sand is made effective by the verdure of the hillside seen beyond.

A ROJI (PASSAGE WAY) OF URASENKE. Urasenke has many *chaseki*, including the
excellent *Konnichian* the term meaning 'tea room of today' referring to the remark made by a Zen priest
to the effect that we know not what may happen tomorrow; we are certain only of today, of this moment.
The date of construction of this minute tea room is not clear, but Horin of Kinkakuji first sipped tea from
a bowl in it on the 25th day of the fifth month, 1648. At the entrance to Urasenke is a beautifully pro-
portioned gate-house.

This is a typical long *roji* of the simple type, imbedded with cobblestones in the 'hail' pattern. It leads
to a bench and still further into inner gardens with various *chaseki*.

81

KATSURA IMPERIAL VILLA GARDEN, KYOTO

82

KATSURA IMPERIAL VILLA GARDEN, KYOTO. The garden of the Katsura Imperial Villa is considered the most beautiful in Japan. Popular tradition has it that it was laid out by Kobori Enshu, who is said to have undertaken the work under three conditions: no limitation to expenses; no limit to time; no interference until completion. But no document so far has been found to show that Enshu has anything to do with it.

The *shin* (or formal) part of the garden shows the *shokin-tei* tea-house, the name suggesting the lyrical music of pine-trees that could be heard in this building.

In order to facilitate the enjoyment of the spacious garden, the path goes up and down the hills, or into the woods or out into the open.

Though harmonious as a whole, the garden may be said to consist of three differently treated parts, of which the northern looks strict and formal: the middle is less so, the southernmost part very simple and informal. It has four *chaseki* each with its own garden. Each of these four gardens is most beautiful in one of the four seasons. The water-basin under the eaves of the *chaseki* is filled with sand when not in use.

SHOKADO'S GARDEN. This was designed by Shokado Shojo on the 18th day of the 9th month, 1639. He was a versatile genius, showing a great talent in calligraphy, painting, *chanoyu*, landscape architecture and flower arrangement as well. He was a friend of Ishikawa Jozan and Sakawada Kiroku. This is a small flat garden with a dry landscape. On the whole the present garden preserves the original layout. It belongs to Mr Toshitaro Nishimura. Area ⅙ acre.

84

GENKYU-EN GARDEN, SHIGA PREFECTURE. From its styles and technique the Genkyu-en is believed to be older than the Rakuraku-en which is situated adjacent to it, and is thought to date from about 1624. The castle, as well as the Genkyu-en and Rakuraku-en, belongs to the Ii family. This garden is one of the largest and best of the Early Edo period. Genkyu can be translated as 'mysterious palace' or 'palace of gods'. There are groups of rocks to represent the crane or tortoise and a large pond to be enjoyed by boat.

OPPOSITE: SHUKKEI-EN, HIROSHIMA. This garden is known also as Sentei (Water Garden) because great importance is given to the pond. It was laid out soon after the feudal lord Asano Nagaakira built his villa here in 1620. Until recent years it was maintained by the Asano family, but recently it was given to the City of Hiroshima. The garden suffered severely from the atomic bomb but the city of Hiroshima has done much to restore it, having replanted more than 5,000 trees or plants. 'The rest of the work may be done by Nature herself. In 50 years or so from now the garden will have recovered, at least in part', remarked the gardener who was taking care of it.

Two slightly arching bridges—one monolithic and the other earthen—meet on a small island where a stone lantern is constructed of natural rocks.

KODAI-JI GARDEN, KYOTO. Work on this garden must have begun about 1620 and it was finished by 1685. The *Chanoyu Hyorin Taisei*, published in 1697, comments on this garden as being the work of 'no common artist', but who he was is not known.

The garden still has crane and tortoise islands symbolizing *Horai*. It seems to have been influenced by a picture of a landscape with stately mansions.

Though this garden is very dilapidated, it has always been looked upon with great interest because of the typical Japanese harmony between garden and buildings. Area slightly over 1 acre.

Outstanding is the stone bridge, the middle portion of which reminds one of the arching bridge in the Koraku-en in Tokyo. On account of this bridge this garden has been said to reproduce Hsi Hu in a miniature scale. Hence it is of the *Shukkei* type. As is usual with gardens of feudal lords, it has hills on the northern side, and a long strip of ground along the western boundary for riding. Two slightly arching bridges—one monolithic and the other earthen—meet on a small island where a stone lantern is constructed of natural rocks.

SHUKKEI-EN, HIROSHIMA

87

RITSURIN-EN, TAKAMATSU. This garden was made by Matsudaira Yorishige, between 1673, and 1745.
A large park at the foot and on the slope of a hill with ponds and bridges, it is of the *kaiyu-shiki* type, to be sauntered in for enjoyment. There are a number of *shoin*, *chaseki* and arbours, which form focal points for the various sections of the garden. The basis of the garden as a whole is *Horai*. All sorts of techniques are employed, notable *shakkei* (the method of 'borrowing' other scenes for the completion of a scenery) and *shukkei*, the method of suggesting well-known scenes by reproducing them in miniature or by using their characteristics, such as the 53 scenes of the highway from Edo to Kyoto, which became fashionable in gardens at this time.

88

The garden shows many excellent examples of clipping and training trees into beautiful forms. Not only among the trees and shrubs but also in the rocks one finds a great variety of rare specimens gathered from various islands of the inland sea. It took the combined efforts of several generations of feudal lords to build this great monument to the people's love of nature. In 1875 it was made a public park and is now maintained as such by Kagawa Prefecture. Area about 39 acres.

RITSURIN-EN, TAKAMATSU

KORAKU-EN GARDEN, TOKYO. Tokugawa Iefusa, Iyeyasu's son, received as a gift from the third Shogun Iemitsu a piece of land in Tokyo (then called Edo). That was in 1629, and within a few days he started to make a garden.

His successor Mitsukuni took over the work with zeal, and with the aid of Chu Shun-shui, a learned visitor from Ming China who was staying with him, infused the garden with something of Chinese taste. The result was a sort of harmony of Japanese and Chinese elements, as evidenced in the pavement of the garden path, and the introduction of Chinese scenes, such as the suggestion of the hills of Lun Shan and the causeway of Hsi Hu, into the garden. The Chinese scholar taught us the secret of the key-stone in the construction of the full moon bridge—a full moon as it forms a circle with its reflection. Trees are always planted nearby the waterfalls so that their branches may conceal a part of them.

Nearly all the buildings in the garden were destroyed in the earthquake and fire of 1923, including one of them dedicated to Saigyo, a mendicant priest poet, leaving only a stone monument bearing one of his verses, which may be rendered thus:

90

KORAKU-EN GARDEN, TOKYO

Along the road by the stream of clear water
  there stands a willow-tree.
  In the shade of it we halt
  but only for a while.
Thus sang the mendicant priest, conscious of the incessant flow of the
water, the weariness of the road we have to travel, and the fleeting joy
of refreshing oneself in the shade. Does our life here consist of nothing
more? Many a visitor to this garden must have asked himself the
question. The wearisome road may not be eternal. May the road lead
us to eternity!

OKAYAMA KORAKU-EN, OKAYAMA. Ikeda Tsunamasa, feudal lord of Okayama, commissioned Tsuda Nagatada to lay out this garden on the northern bank of the River Asahi on the opposite bank to Okayama castle. The work was started in 1687, some four acres were added in 1690 and later it was again increased to its present size.

This garden has many points similar to others maintained by feudal lords in the Edo period, but differs from them in details. For instance, there is this huge rock forming a precipitous bank of the pond at the south-west corner of the garden. The rock was found on Inushima island in the Inland Sea but was too large to be transported in one piece. So it was smashed into 96 pieces and reconstructed here in its original form. There is another huge rock which was transported in 30 pieces and reconstructed in this garden to suggest the huge crag of Ishiyamadera. Area about 21 acres.

OPPOSITE: IMPERIAL GIFT PARK IN SHIBA, TOKYO. This is called the *Onshiko-en* which means Imperial gift park. It is the garden of the former Shiba Detached Palace and was given to the City of Tokyo after the great earthquake and fire of 1923, in commemoration of the Emperor's wedding.

When the garden was first laid out about 250 years ago it was on the seashore and commanded an extensive view of Shinagawa Bay. Not only had the garden the advantage of the view of the sea as a background, but also within it the ebb and flow of the tide was utilized by connecting the pond in the garden

with the sea. Such a device was not altogether peculiar to this garden; in others of the Edo period similar uses of the sea were made. But here the landscape architects took further advantage of the sea in the construction of the garden. Stepping stones were laid out in the pond so as to be invisible at high tide but visible at low tide when one could step along them and reach the island. When the land adjacent to this garden was reclaimed in recent years, the connection of the pond with the sea had to be severed.

93

GARDEN OF THE FORMER
HAMA PALACE, TOKYO.

The site of this garden has had a long and interesting history. The area had been a swamp used by the Shoguns as their hawking ground, and in 1664 the garden was brought into being when a stone wall was erected on the landward side.

The whole estate was handed over to the Emperor in 1868 when the Shogun stepped down and power was restored to the throne. The site is now an island, almost square in shape, protected by stone embankments all around, exposed to the sea on the south-east and surrounded by moats on the other three sides. About six and a half acres are occupied by a lake containing three islands. Bridges across the pond are covered with wisteria arbours.

Hidden from the garden proper by groves of trees are two duck hunting enclosures. The larger one occupies about 10 acres and the smaller about 4 acres. These hunting ponds in the Hama Detached Palace have been in use for more than 160 years. The novelty of catching ducks with hand-nets and then feasting on them afterwards at a *sukiyaki* dinner in one of the tea-houses in the garden has always furnished fine entertainment for foreign guests.

The garden was given to the City of Tokyo in 1945, to be maintained as a public park.

94

SEISHU-EN GARDEN,
KUMAMOTO.

This is better known as the Suizenji garden because a temple of that name formerly occupied the site. The garden was opened to the public soon after the Restoration in 1868. The large pond, with its wonderfully clear flowing water, reflecting promontories and islands, may be encircled by the visitor along paths which give varied and interesting views at every turn. An artificial hill shaped like Fujiyama is conspicuous at the west end of the garden.

There are two bridges: one in front of a shrine and the other at the east side of the base of Fujiyama. Conspicuous are the stepping stones (*sawa-tobi*) laid in the water across the pond and joining two islands. This is a feature seldom seen in gardens, and affords an opportunity for visitors to appreciate the beauty of the crystalline water, for which it is famous.

6. MIDDLE EDO (1681-1778)

AT the beginning of this period, Tsunayoshi (1680–1708) was Shogun. Being a devout Buddhist, he had established or rebuilt many temples and did much to encourage the development of gardens. But the gardens of temples had since the Momoyama period very little, if any, religious elements in them. To be sure, certain religious symbols such as *Sanzon-seki* (*trinity rocks*) continued to be placed in the garden but merely by empty tradition. The whole emphasis was placed on the beauty of the garden.

Yoshimune the 8th Tokugawa Shogun (1716–1744), was frugal in his policy and warned the people against all extravagance. In consequence no more large-scale gardens such as those made in the previous period were constructed while he was in power. Yet the extravagant habits of the people were not easily crushed. While they observed the law and kept their gardens as small as possible they did their best to improve their quality so as to increase their enjoyment when they gazed at them. To that end more attention came to be paid to the trees and other minor details of the garden.

We must not ignore another outstanding reason for making small-scale gardens during this period, which was that there was almost no garden construction by feudal lords. In the Early Edo period great feudal lords had vied with each other in constructing enormous gardens in order to maintain their dignity or prestige. But now, after the battle of Seki-gahara, peace was restored to the nation and there was no need for self-advertisement. There were some rich landowners and wealthy merchants who might have had large gardens, but they were not allowed to.

Secrets in the art of garden construction, known as *ku-den*, denoting a thing not to be written down but to be transmitted from mouth to ear, came to assume great importance in this period. Even so, hardly any trace of them remains in the gardens still available to us. Because of limited size, many things which were in the larger gardens had to be simplified or omitted. One of the first things to disappear from the garden was the waterfall. It was replaced by a stream and a rock composition depicting a dry waterfall. The Horai type garden continued to be made, but hardly ever were independent crane and tortoise islands made. These islands were often reduced in size or merely suggested by a peninsula or by the use of a rock composition on the bank. Frequently they disappeared from the garden altogether without leaving any trace.

Another peculiarity of the garden of this period was the use of only small stones, but in great numbers, the whole giving an impression of weakness, and mention may be made of the clipping of trees, some being rounded and others square-topped.

There was a strong tendency to overcrowd the garden with stone lanterns. They had been introduced into the garden primarily for use, to provide light at night and also, though incidentally, for decorative effect.

GYOKUSEN-EN, KANAZAWA. This garden appears in a map of the Empo era (1673–1680) in which its present plan may already be recognized, in spite of later alterations. It is now in the possession of Mr Giichiro-Nishimura. The garden consists of upper and lower levels with a pond on the upper level and a larger pond below at the foot of the steep hillside, the two ponds being joined by a waterfall and a stream. The garden is provided with paths which enable one to saunter in it and enjoy its various beautiful aspects. At the same time it may be appreciated from the *chaseki* and guest-room, so well utilized is the steep hillside which is thickly wooded with ancient trees, a true sylvan solitude of profound serenity. The special kind of rocks peculiar to Noto peninsula with crackled effects are used in profusion. Area about 1 acre.

RINNO-JI GARDEN, NIKKO. This garden seems to have been laid out originally as early as 1244. but Rinno-ji was moved to the present site in 1648, burned down in 1684 and reconstructed two years later. The garden may rightly be considered to have been laid out about this time, though merely a trace of the work of that period may now be found, because of the great remodelling which took place in 1815.

There are some stone lanterns in three- or five-roofed *stupa* shapes, the use of which is confined to the Early and Middle Edo periods. The use of these lanterns, together with clipped bushes and groups of rocks, greatly enhances the effect the garden has on visitors. Area about $\frac{3}{5}$ acre.

OPPOSITE: RIKUGI-EN GARDEN, TOKYO. The term *Rikugi* denotes the six varieties into which Chinese and Japanese poetry have been classified. In addition 88 names of places famous for their scenic beauty referred to in famous Japanese verses are used to designate different places in the garden. Because of these intimate connections with literature, it is rightly called the Garden of Poetry. It was completed in 1702, after seven-and-a-half years of assiduous designing and close supervision by Yanagisawa Yoshiyasu, a trusted minister of the Shogun Tsuneyoshi.

When it fell into the hands of Baron Iwasaki soon after the Restoration of the Imperial powers in 1868, the garden was carefully restored according to the original drawing and description of the garden left by Yanagisawa himself. In 1938 Baron Iwasaki donated the garden to the City of Tokyo.

Rikugi-en is so laid out as to be enjoyed by persons strolling about in it. Under old spreading camphor and gingko-trees are found suitable places for introspection and meditation. It has a large lake which is still fed by the Senkawa water system. The lake represents an ocean with many beautiful inlets and with a large island, representing Horai. The bridge seen to the right leads on to the Elysian island still with a number of old pine trees. The shadows of the leaves make an interesting pattern on the ground. The other views above, show a glimpse of Atami-no Chaya and a vine-covered stone lantern. Area about 25 acres.

98

RIKUGI-EN GARDEN, TOKYO

KISSUI-EN, KAKE, HIROSHIMA PREFECTURE. After travelling among mountains for
two long hours from Hiroshima on a shaking bus, I came upon Kissui-en in its secluded valley thickly
wooded with cryptomerea and camphor trees of great age. It has been carefully maintained by an ancient
Kake family. Its perfect tranquillity at once drew me close to nature. I was deeply struck by the ingenious
way the natural scenery was 'borrowed' in order to give expanse to the garden. An island can be seen in
the pond : it is connected by a stone bridge and decorated with a stone stupa.

On the slope of the hill I found a stone monument, erected to commemorate the 500th anniversary of
the founding of the family, the garden itself having been started in 1781 and finished two years later. About
5 years after that it was improved and remodelled by an expert gardener from Kyoto.

KISSUI-EN, KAKE,
HIROSHIMA PREFECTURE

KANSUI-EN GARDEN: WASEDA UNIVERSITY, TOKYO. The importance of learning has always been emphasized in Japan, and especially since World War II every learned institution in the country has been struggling to accommodate the ever-increasing numbers of students. Waseda University is no exception. New buildings are being put up in every available space, but more are required, in spite of rigid entrance examinations and the soaring cost of living and tuition.

To cope with this problem many things have to be sacrificed. Only a few days ago I visited the Kansui-en garden, situated a few blocks away from the Waseda University campus, and was confronted with what I thought was a serious problem from the cultural standpoint. The university has already turned a large proportion of an old estate into athletic fields, including an archery range, and a number of students were using an old landscape garden as a place to rest. I was glad to find no sign of maltreatment of this beautiful garden. It has a grove of ancient trees and well-designed ponds on two levels: shown here is the rapids where water of the upper pond flows into the lower. Let us hope it will be preserved for quiet meditation.

102

GARDEN OF FUMON-IN, TOFUKU-JI, KYOTO. The present garden is believed to have been laid out early in the Middle Edo period, though some modifications must have been made in 1827 when the Fumon-in temple was reconstructed. A greater change in the garden was made in 1877 when it was divided by a stone pavement leading to the Founder's Hall, separating the part with the pond from that with the dry landscape which is flat and covered with beautifully raked sand, which has crane and tortoise islands with trees and a rock composition. The lower view is across this sand garden towards the temple gate-house. It is thus a combination of the garden of a Zen temple with another type suitable for a warrior's *shoin*.

7. LATE EDO (1779-1868)

IN the face of national economic difficulties, hardly any garden worth mentioning was constructed during this period, either among the people or for temples and shrines. To be sure there were some exceptions, but they were very few. Among these exceptions the most conspicuous was the Kenroku Park at Kanazawa which is still maintained as one of the four great gardens of Japan.

Under these circumstances it is interesting to note that a number of gardeners who had some experience in Edo went from place to place in the country, calling themselves *niwashi* (gardeners) and teaching what they called the 'secrets of the art of garden making'. Some went even to Kyushu and laid out gardens there. They were welcomed in different parts of the country and helped to spread the mistaken idea that there were strict and fast rules for making a garden, the knowledge of which was essential to any who wished to do such work. What with the restrictions which were placed upon the people by various economic difficulties and the respect they paid to strict rules which they believed existed but which ignored the fundamental laws of nature and brought decadence to the garden art, it was impossible for the garden to make any substantial progress, except perhaps towards omitting details and general simplification, if that can be called progress

OPPOSITE: KENROKU-EN, KANAZAWA. A garden was started here in 1676, centring about a lotus pond, but the Kenroku-en in its present form was completed during the period 1822–1840. With the end of the feudal system, the garden ceased to be possessed by the Maeda family and in 1874 it was opened to the public as a park, being given the name Kenroku-en (garden of the sextuple combination). This indicates that the park combines six prominent features, namely: vastness, solemnity, endeavour, venerability, abundant supply of water and superb views.

Great ingenuity is shown in getting water into this garden. The feudal lord Toshitsune was much worried about the scarcity of water in his castle moat and commissioned Itaya Heishiro to solve the problem. He succeeded in leading the water from the river about 5 miles away and forcing it up the hill into the park by applying the principle of the siphon. This engineering feat still works to perfection.

The Kenroku Garden is one of the four most beautiful landscape gardens in Japan, the other three being the Tokiwa-en of Mito, the Ritsurin-en of Takamatsu, and the Koraku-en of Okayama. Seen here is a bridge designed to suggest the flight of a flock of geese, and the famous two-legged stone lantern described as koto-bridge design. Area about 24 acres.

NANKO GARDEN, SHIRAKAWA, FUKUSHIMA PREFECTURE

OPPOSITE: NANKO GARDEN, SHIRAKAWA, FUKUSHIMA-KEN. This park was established by Matsudaira Sadanobu (1757–1829) master of Shirakawa Castle, an outstanding statesman of the Tokugawa regime. At the same time he was a man of culture, with special talent for making gardens. He created a lake, about half-a-mile long and almost half as wide, out of a swamp and used it as a reservoir for the irrigation of farm land. It was used for boating and paths were built to enable people to go around it and enjoy the view. A few small buildings including the *kyoraku-tei* (pavilion of shared pleasure) were put up for the people to rest in.

There are clumps of pine-trees and avenues of cherry and maple-trees, which provide different attractions for different seasons of the year. The garden was beautiful in snow when the author visited it.

GARDEN IN KANAZAWA, formerly the property of Mr Honda but now attached to the Hokkoku Kaikan. The garden has been very much neglected of late, but the large pond still keeps a dignity of its own. It has an island on the further side with a *stupa* and a dignified worshipping rock in the foreground close to the water's edge. In it there still lingers the serenity of feudal Japan.

SEISONKAKU GARDEN, KANAZAWA. The Seisonkaku was built in 1863 for the mother of the Lord of Kanazawa and is situated south of the Kenroku-en. It has a flat garden to be enjoyed from a *chanoyu* room named Kikakutei (flying crane). This still has a hexagonal water-basin decorated with six Jizo in relief, and also a stone lantern similarly decorated, all brought from Edo. The interesting feature of this garden is that in it is a *kyokusui* (winding stream) which leads into the building before it winds its way through the garden into the pond and finally tumbles down the waterfall into the lower pond in the Kenroku-en.

GARDEN OF ENGAKU-JI, KAMAKURA. One of the five important Buddhist temples of Kamakura, and established in 1282, Engaku-ji has a small neglected garden behind the main temple. It has a pond with stepping stones and a tiny stone bridge spanning a part of the pond which is partially enclosed by a peninsula.

Seen above is another garden on the other side of the fence and road, featuring a large rectangular pond shaded by a gigantic camphor-tree and other aged trees growing on the hillside sloping down to the pond. It is situated between the main hall of Engaku-ji and the Hall of Meditation.

These two gardens are ancient according to the temple tradition, but some specialists disagree and are of the opinion that they are of a much later period.

KOTO-IN GARDEN, KYOTO. The garden of this temple is different from those of others in that it has more freedom and resemblance to nature; it is flat and wooded, conspicuous for the absence of ornaments of any kind except young trees.

This is the temple where Hosokawa Yusai's tomb is located. His tombstone is unique being no other than a stone lantern of which he was very fond. So strongly was he attached to it that he always had his men carry it back and forth between his home and Edo, hundreds of miles away, when the terms of his service required his presence there.

GARDEN OF SEISEN PRIMARY SCHOOL, KAMAKURA. It was some time ago that I heard of the garden which belonged to the house once occupied by Yoritomo, founder of the Kamakura regime, but it was not until recently that I visited it. It is at Nikaido, close to his tomb, and is used as a playground by the recently opened Seisen Girls Primary School. I have been unable to investigate its authenticity, but I am giving it a little space and wondering what will be the influence upon young minds of a garden with such a tradition.

SHUKO'S CHASEKI GARDEN, NARA. Murato Shuko (1421–1502) originator of the simplified *chanoyu* which was later perfected by Senno Rikyu, was once a priest of the Shomyo-ji in Nara. In this temple is a *chaseki*, which is said to have been built years ago in accordance with Shuko's ideas. It has a little garden containing his tomb. Here is a glimpse of that garden from the *chaseki*, showing a well and a *tsukubai*, or basin for handwashing.

112

LOTUS POND OF KONCHI-IN, KYOTO. The exact date of this garden is unknown. It occupies the northern corner of the rectangular piece of land mostly taken up by the crane and tortoise garden in front of the *hojo* of Konchi-in, and the contrast of the two is very interesting, the young buds of lotus suggesting an ethereal music by an orchestra.

8. SINCE THE RESTORATION

WITH the restoration of power to the Imperial throne in 1868, the feudal system of Japan nominally came to an end, and western civilization poured into the country. For a time it was the cry of the age to destroy every institution which had no counterpart in the civilized west. Many European-style edifices came to be built, and in 1873 the government decided to establish public parks throughout the country for the recreation of the people. In Tokyo the following five places were designated as parks before the end of that year: the precinct of the Asakusa Temple, the precinct of Zojo-ji at Shiba; the grounds of Kanei-ji, still maintained as Ueno Park and Zoo; the grounds of the Tomioka Hachiman shrine; Asukayama, still famous for its cherry blossom. Other cities throughout the country followed suit and Tokyo itself added more to the list. Quite a number of large Japanese gardens belonging to the Imperial family, or those in the possession of former feudal lords or wealthy persons, and sites of ancient castles in different parts of the country, have been turned into public parks.

The development of Japanese gardens since the Kamakura period had often been connected with the temples, but it took a different course after the restoration. Now it was to be seen in the mansions and villas of the wealthy upon the one hand and in the small gardens of middle-class people on the other.

As was the case with many forms of art in this period, gardens were made in the various styles of different countries of the west. But there came times of reaction against foreign culture, especially after the war against China and Russia, when the traditional Japanese style came to be strongly upheld above all others.

A study of the great number of gardens created throughout the country during this period shows there were the following three types: (1) imitative, either of European gardens, or the traditional style; (2) idealistic, using a pictorial or symbolic style; (3) naturalistic, combining eastern and western elements. Of these, the naturalistic type of mainly Japanese elements enjoyed the greatest favour, particularly the type known as *shakkei-shiki*. This was easier in the gardens of Kyoto surrounded as it is by mountains. In a city like Tokyo where no mountains were in sight, it was difficult to 'borrow' natural scenes. Nevertheless great efforts were made to recreate nature in one's garden by taking advantage of every available means.

Before the Restoration, all gardens were planned with a religious background, though it may have been merely in form and verging on the superstitious in many cases. After the Restoration the religious background was abandoned and efforts were made to base garden construction on aesthetics pure and simple. Formerly, what was lacking in the art was made up by the religious fervour of those who designed and supervised gardens. But now without such a fervour, they were left in the hands of the *niwashi* or unexperienced novices, and the result was shown in a product which lacked dignity and profundity. To be sure some of the gardens were quite spacious and not without merit in certain features such as the use of water in streams, but they were especially weak in the use of rocks and rock composition. It may be said that the gardens of Japan are now in the transitional and experimental period. The greatest problem seems to lie in creating a special type of garden to harmonize with the European or semi-European style of architecture of many Japanese dwelling houses.

114

MURIN-AN GARDEN, KYOTO. This garden was completed in 1894 by Ogawa Jihei under the close supervision of the late Prince Yamagata. The garden is laid out on a gentle slope. At the top it has a cascade with water falling in three stages and flowing into a small pond which feeds a stream. This was made to meander down the gentle slope and is joined by another stream further down. It is one of the best gardens of the Meiji era. One may saunter in the garden and derive great pleasure from it, but it is appreciated best from the guest room further down the slope.

When the garden was nearing completion, Prince Yamagata is reported to have commented that the gardeners of his day were too much inclined towards seclusion and loneliness in their gardens but that he wanted to have something more audacious. So he gave more life to the trees and more force to the running water. Looking up to the thick growth of trees he felt the suggestion of solitude. Looking down into the depth of water in the pond he felt the spirit of audacity. In order to get these effects he brought into his garden, small as it is, a rock which required a team of more than 20 oxen to draw it from its bed many miles away. Area about ¾ acre.

Roji of Chaseki on TAKAGA-MINE, outside KYOTO. The Honnami family had for generations followed the profession of testing and sharpening swords. Honnami Koetsu (1558–1637) showed unusual talent, not only in this profession, but also in calligraphy, painting, and lacquer and ceramics. He excelled in the simple refinement of *chanoyu*. The tea bowls he made in his own kiln are considered among the most important tea utensils existing today. Late in life, Koetsu received as a gift from Ieyasu a tract of land on Takaga-mine, a hill in the outskirts of Kyoto. Here he assembled artists of various crafts, one of each, and tried to form a Koetsu Village. He still has a large number of followers who hold an annual *chanoyu* meeting on Takaga-mine when they exhibit and use *chanoyu* utensils made by him. This meeting is considered a great occasion for the art-lovers of the nation, who gather on this hill for the aesthetic enjoyment of the day. Shown here is a glimpse of a *chaseki* with a bamboo fence.

OPPOSITE: GARDEN OF THE HEIAN SHRINE, KYOTO. Kyoto was founded as the capital of Japan in 794 and remained so for nearly eleven centuries. In commemoration of the 1100th anniversary of the founding of the city, the Heian Shrine was built in 1895 and a garden was laid out to an elaborate plan. It consists of the East garden, centring about the *Seihochi* (Phoenix Pond), the Central garden about the *Seiryu-chi* (Blue Dragon Pond), and the West garden about the *Byakko-chi* (White Tiger Pond). Of these the West garden and then the Central garden were the first to be completed, though some of the work took years to complete. Instead of a bridge, what is known to Japanese gardeners as *sawa-watari* (stepping stones) was created, mainly with old stone pillars of the bridge. The entire garden was designed and executed by Ogawa Jihei. It features lakes and it can be appreciated by sauntering along the paths, or by using a boat. The garden as a whole is in the Horai style. Variations at different seasons of the year were sought and achieved, and distant views are freely 'borrowed'. Area about 5 acres.

116

TENJU-AN GARDEN, KYOTO. Tenju-an, a tributary temple of Nanzen-ji, was first established as early as 1338 and was re-established by Hosokawa Yusai when he rebuilt the *hojo* in 1607; the garden was re-modelled in 1904–5 by the priest Kozan Kyosa, who possessed unusual talent in garden making. That is the reason why the present Tenju-an, while retaining elements of the *kaiyu* style in the old garden, also possesses those of the *kansho* style in the new, with stepping stones, clipped bushes and large rock compositions.

OPPOSITE: MR ICHIDA'S GARDEN, KYOTO. On the site of an old temple this garden was laid out about 1879, and acquired by Mr Ichida in 1892. Drastic changes were begun by his successor in 1907. The design and execution of the remodelling were undertaken by Ogawa Jihei. One of the peculiarities of this period, it may be noted, was to have the garden start at a higher elevation than the house and slope downward. 'Borrowed' landscapes, too, were popular.

In many respects this is a typical Japanese garden for a *shoin*, and it combines the sauntering element with the *kansho* element, the latter influencing the design by requiring the whole garden to be visible from one spot. An abundant supply of water is made to flow into streams, collect into a pond and flow down again into the lower pond. Area about 1 acre.

119

MR FUJIYAMA'S GARDEN, TOKYO. The present garden was first designed by the late Mr Raita-Fujiyama about 1899 and executed by the gardener Matsumoto-Kamekichi. But each time a new addition was made to the house it necessitated a modification of the garden. There is now a terrace in front of the European-style architecture, a Japanese *shoin* style garden to go with the traditional style house, and there are *roji* for the *chaseki* in various places in the garden. There exist many large representative gardens in Tokyo, but one shortcoming is their scarcity of water, in contrast to the gardens of Kyoto where an abundant supply is obtained from the canal which draws it from Lake Biwa. In this one is a stream which skirts the base of the spacious lawn and flows into a small but interesting pond. Area about 3 acres.

120

MR SAIGO'S GARDEN, TOKYO. This was originally attached to Mr Nakagawa's residence, and the garden laid out in the Early Edo period still exists, though much remodelling was done after the property was taken over by Marquis Saigo in 1871 and a European-style house built. There is a spacious lotus pond with a few bronze cranes.

MR TSUJI'S GARDEN, KANAZAWA. Mr Tsuji has built his home on an edge of the plateau on the bank of the River Saikawa where he has a clear view up the river into the distant mountains. He has had his garden built on the precipice and at the bottom of it is a pond fed by a natural spring on the steep slope.

OPPOSITE: MR INAHATA'S GARDEN, KYOTO. This is one of the large gardens of Kyoto and enjoys an abundant supply of water, which forms a waterfall, collects in a pond and flows in streams. The picture was taken early in May, about the time of the *tango* (boys' festival) observed on the fifth day of the fifth month of the year, when the homes where there are boys hoist paper carps at the top of a bamboo pole. The custom is based on the tradition that the carp, which is regarded as a *samurai* fish because it never flinches when placed on the carving board, swims against the strong current of the river and jumps up cataracts. When it succeeds in jumping up the cataract called 'Dragon Gate' it becomes a dragon. The dragon in the Far East is considered an almighty being, and for the carp to become a dragon signifies great success in life. Therefore, when fond parents hoist the paper-made carps, it signifies their earnest hope that their sons will be as successful in life as the carps.

123

123

MR MINAMI'S GARDEN, KANAZAWA. Granite rocks with crackled effect, known as *Taki-ishi* found in the Noto peninsula, are used extensively in the Kanazawa region. Its pleasing texture harmonizes well with other kinds and gives the feeling of age and wear, and it affords a place for mosses to grow. The crackled effect is due to the constant beating of the rough sea. A slightly arching stone bridge with railings, across the narrow portion of the pond, gives character to this garden. A number of different types of stone lanterns and water-basins are indispensable. One of the water-basins is here shown with a roof-shaped cover to protect the water from falling leaves.

MR HAYASHIYA'S GARDEN, KANAZAWA. Kanazawa is known for its great humidity, and it interested me very much to find moss cultivated here in the house proper behind glass sliding doors, stepping stones being led into the house. Here the garden comes literally into the house. There is a group of three large pine-trees growing outside almost at the edge of the garden; they are only about 30 feet high but their branches spread out as if from one trunk, shading a distance of no less than 120 feet.

GARDEN OF YOSHINOYA, YAMANAKA. The hotel was built on the edge of the gorge projecting from, or almost overhanging, the precipice so that the occupants of the inn may look down upon the gushing river that strikes a rock and turns and returns as willed by nature, as shown here. The large entrance opens to the road, but is partially concealed from passers-by by a small wooded 'island' with rock-work.

GARDEN OF YATAYA HOT SPRING INN, KATAYAMATSU. The hotel was built on the edge of Katayamatsu Bay, and the garden is laid out along the water's edge so as to suggest that the bay, with its peninsulas and boats, belongs to the garden. The famous two-legged stone lantern of the Kenroku-en was copied for this garden. Part of the house was built on stilts to provide for exceptionally high tides, and a stretch of the waterfront was turned into a private landing place.

GARDEN OF YOSHINOYA'S ANNEX, YAMANAKA. The annex is situated on the hillside across the road from the main house of Yoshinoya. It consisted of several small independent houses built on the hillside, but recently the Shimizu Kensetsu completed the scheme of connecting these traditional style houses by means of covered corridors, and to the main hotel by means of elevators and a tunnel under the road. The greatest care was taken not to spoil the natural beauty in the construction.

MR YAGI'S GARDEN, KYOTO. A *shakkei* type garden, having successfully incorporated all the hills of Kyoto as the background of the pond. Its beautiful details may be appreciated by sauntering through the garden which has two or three *chaseki* with charming approaches with *tsukubai* (stone water-basins). This is the view eastward from one of the *chaseki*.

129

ISUI-EN (MR SEKI'S GARDEN) NARA. Isui-en, the most famous Japanese garden in Nara, generally means the old garden in front of the Sanshu-tei (made as early as the 1670's by Kiyosumi Doshin of Nara) together with Isui-en proper laid out about 1897 by a gardener named Uye-zen. The present master of the house has also contributed toward the perfection of the garden: the grass-covered knoll in the middle distance was lowered about two feet, and another knoll was created beyond that, so as to introduce the distant hill of Wakakusa-yama. Thus the famous hills and peaks round about Nara, as well as the Nandai-mon Gate (built in the Kamakura period) of the Todaiji were 'borrowed'. It is now one of the most representative, large-scale Japanese gardens as developed in the Meiji era (1868–1912). A gate to a *chaseki*: the small stone on the stepping stone indicates that the passage is closed. Area about 2 acres.

130

MR HARA'S GARDEN, GOTENYAMA, TOKYO. While sauntering in this garden, one would hardly ever be disturbed by the noise of the trains that frequently pass close by, so far away one feels himself to be from the world. As soon as one enters through the gate into the garden one feels himself in an entirely different world. A sandy path leads the wanderer into interesting places in the garden adorned by rare stone lanterns of Japanese and Korean origin. A lily pond further down is very impressive with the feeling of remoteness from the hustle and bustle of this world which it creates. Various types of stone lanterns are used; here is a Korean type.

OKUMA KAIKAN'S GARDEN, TOKYO

The house in which Count Okuma, the founder of Waseda University lived stood close to the main entrance of the University. A new smaller building was put up in place of the older one burned in the late war, and a new garden laid out with a winding stream and an open space of lawn immediately in front of the building. The garden was so planned as to be appreciated from the house, used as the faculty club, or in sauntering through it. One corner was turned into an iris pond with a *yukimi* type stone lantern.

132

One of Mr Tsutsumi's hobbies is garden making. He has been collecting large rocks from distant places for a number of years. A good-sized area in Azabu, Tokyo, was dug up some 30 to 40 feet deep and a garden was planned in it. The garden consists of a rock composition for cataract, a gravelled beach and a pond with bridges. In all appearance the garden is nearly complete, but there is a number of large rocks on rollers still waiting for their final resting places. Now that, with the change of government, he has stepped out of the busy office of the Speaker of the House of Representatives, he may find time to complete his garden.

MR TSUTSUMI'S GARDEN, TOKYO

THE KIYOSUMI GARDEN, TOKYO in Fukagawa Ward was one of the most representative of Japanese gardens in Tokyo when it was planned and its construction directed by Baron Yataro Iwasaki mainly for the purpose of entertaining his guests and affording recreation to the employees of his company. After his death the work on the garden was finished by his brother in 1891.

In 1920 Baron Iwasaki felt the condition of the world had changed. He had one corner of the garden, about 2½ acres, turned into a children's playground and tennis court for public use.

134

THE KIYOSUMI GARDEN,
TOKYO

A full view of Kiyosumi-en from the top of the hill in the garden. In this garden more than 15,000 people are said to have taken refuge and thus saved their lives at the time of the great earthquake and fire of 1923. In that catastrophe all the buildings, except one, were consumed by fire and many rare trees were destroyed. It was then that Baron Iwasaki made up his mind to sacrifice the western half of the garden and present the eastern half, which was comparatively little damaged, to the City of Tokyo. His deed of gift emphasized his desire that people tired from their work might here come in contact with nature and so refresh their minds and preserve their health. Though small compared with the original, the present garden is nevertheless to be counted as one of the largest and most beautiful in Tokyo.

135

OPPOSITE: OLD SHINJUKU IMPERIAL GARDEN, TOKYO. This garden was opened to the public in May 1949 as the Shinjuku National Park Garden (Kokumin Koen Shinjuku Gyoen). Its kaleidoscopic history of nearly 350 years epitomises the history of Japan itself over the same period.

In 1900 Mr Fukuba commissioned a French landscape architect, Henry Martinet, to design a garden for Shinjuku. The plan for this European-style garden was executed under the supervision of Mr Fukuba himself and completed in 1906. There is also a Japanese-style garden covering about 25 acres and designed by Yoshichika Kodaira, in pleasing contrast to the 'foreign' garden, the two being so laid out as to reveal the best in each. While the latter is at its best in the spring when cherries are in full bloom, the European garden reveals its deepest charm, perhaps, in autumn when maple leaves show all the colours of a beautiful brocade.

Being screened off by a thick coat of gingko, cypress, maples and pines, the Japanese garden gives a sense of seclusion. With an atmosphere of sylvan solitude, the ponds give the impression of being located in the heart of mountains. In the westernmost part, there is a large pond with bridges. This used to be the duck-hunting pond and the woods behind it create a deep shadow on the water, especially at sunset, bringing nature close to us.

SANKEI-EN GARDEN, YOKOHAMA. The name means 'Garden of Three Valleys' and being close to the sea, the garden is provided with swimming and boating facilities.

On the top of one of the hills stands a three-storeyed stupa, which is considered to date from about the fifteenth century in the Muromachi period. It was brought from the Tomyo-ji temple in Kyoto and re-erected here about 40 years ago. It is scheduled as an important cultural property.

OLD SHINJUKU IMPERIAL GARDEN, TOKYO

PRINCE SHIMAZU'S
GARDEN,
KAGOSHIMA

TINY GARDEN BY IWAKUNI BRIDGE which serves as a background for the garden laid out on the river bank close to the bridge. It is enlivened by the bridge and the range of mountains in the distance, especially in the rain as when this picture was taken.

OPPOSITE: PRINCE SHIMAZU'S GARDEN, KAGOSHIMA. The stream which flows close by Prince Shimazu's home is led into the pond which is featured in his garden. The garden extends further to the shore and 'borrows' volcanic Sakurajima for the scenic effect of the garden. There is a forest just behind the Shimazu mansion from which a large camphor-tree was felled with proper Buddhist ceremony for sculpting *Goddess of Mercy*, the exact replica of Kudara Kwannon, in the Horyu-ji Monastery. The replica was made by Niiro Chunosuke and now stands in the British Museum, London.

GARDEN OF SHINONOME RESTAURANT, KUMAMOTO. An extensive and elaborate Japanese-style garden of the early Meiji period is shown here. It contains a model of Fuji mountain and a long bridge. The establishment was made famous when Geisha girls went on strike for higher fees and better treatment in the early Meiji era, when such a labour movement was still very rare.

PRINCE SAIONJI'S GARDEN, KYOTO. The garden in its general feature is flat though not without one or two small artificial hills. The south-east of the house is open to a lawn and a pond with an earthen bridge. There is a beautifully composed *tsukubai* and a poetic *chaseki* named *Hoshin-an* (Truth preserving hermitage).

Some feeling of detachment from the world and of close affinity to nature prevails here.

THE CHINZANSO GARDEN, TOKYO

OPPOSITE: THE CHINZANSO GARDEN, TOKYO. This garden was originally designed by Prince Yamagata when he had his villa here and the original plan has been retained to a large measure. The natural contour of land, the hill with a 3-storey stupa on top, the natural spring and pond in the valley, has been utilized to the greatest advantage in the layout. Recently picturesque small houses have been built for the use of various kinds of meetings and repasts and there are many stone monuments and *tsukubai*.

MR SUMITOMO'S GARDEN, KYOTO. The abundance of water in this garden is a great blessing. A large waterfall gushing down from the thickly wooded hill, and the stepping stones of irregular shapes artistically arranged in the water, all give the feeling of being in the heart of nature.

GARDEN OF TOKYO NATIONAL MUSEUM

144

GARDEN OF TOKYO NATIONAL MUSEUM. The present garden in the rear of the museum was laid out when the new building was erected in place of the old after the earthquake of 1923. Formerly there was a dry landscape garden, but it was replaced by the present one which features a pond. The museum, as well as some 81,000 pieces of artistic and historic value, originally constituted the Imperial Household Museum, but they were handed over to the nation when the new constitution was promulgated in 1942.

Details include this water-basin in *futatsu tomoe* design, symbolising the two great elements of positive and negative, principles of the universe.

ROKUSOAN GARDEN, TOKYO. A *chaseki* with six windows (that is what Rokusoan means) was originally built by Kanamori Sowa in 1368 for Jigan-in, a tributary temple of the Kofuku-ji monastery in Nara. The garden was laid out by Kohitsu Ryochu after the *chaseki* was rebuilt with what material remained after the shipwreck off Kishu when it was being transported to Tokyo by boat: it is now in the rear garden of the Tokyo National Museum. The *tsukubai* with Buddhist images carved in relief on the four sides adds dignity to the garden and a few stone lanterns of rare types including the one called *obake* (ghost) lantern bearing the date 16th day, 8th month, 2nd year Keicho (1597) make the garden interesting. In winter there are straw hats for the water-basin and stone lantern, and a bamboo pole supports ropes to relieve the weight of snow on a tree.

The building seen above is a roofed bench called *koshikake*, a necessary edifice easily accessible from the *roji* to be used by the guests to rest during the intermission after the meal before tea is served. The intermission will give enough time for the host to tidy up the room and rearrange things in it so as to give a fresh impression when guests return to the room to continue with tea. The *chaseki*, not shown here, is located close to the *tsukubai* and the views shown here are seen from the *chaseki*.

GARDEN OF SEIZANSO, NEAR MITO. A quiet country place to which Tokugawa Mit-sukuni (1628–1700) retired and devoted the remainder of his life for the compilation of the *History of Japan*. The room with a circular window is said to have been used by him for study. Behind the small hills shown in the garden is the pond which was said to have been designed in the shape of the Chinese character for 'heart', reversed.

HARADA'S
OKUGETSUAN GARDEN,
TOKYO

Volcanic lava from Idzu Peninsula was used for the sides of the front approach to give the visitor an impression of walking up the dry river-bed when approaching the front door and the scheme was carried into the inner garden where a stream was created to flow into a small pond. We have an aged cherry-tree growing so close that, from the house, we are unable to see the blossoms on the branches. We only catch a glimpse of them blooming over the roof of our *chaseki* when entering the front gate. So we wanted to have the water running in the garden in order that we may observe from the room the scattering petals floating down the stream.

Before World War II we tried to change our garden during the winter, when we had our pond covered with a wooden floor and that covered with sand, turning the whole into the dry landscape seen here. The bluish rock with white streaks, coming from the Iyo province in Shikoku, looks very effective.

INNER GARDEN OF MEIJI SHRINE. The topography of the place, its hills, valleys and ponds were utilized to the greatest advantage by Yoshichika Kodaira who designed this garden as well as the Japanese-style garden of Shinjuku. The clipped azalea bushes look wonderful in their season, but the masterpiece of the garden is in the creation of a mighty river of iris flowers winding along the base of hills for which the garden is renowned.

It is recorded that this garden was laid out at the suggestion of Emperor Meiji, who especially wanted the Empress Dowager to enjoy walking in it. For that reason the Emperor was very much concerned about the paths made in the garden.

HIFUKUSHO MEMORIAL GARDEN, TOKYO. In the great earthquake and fire of 1923 more than 60,000 people were trapped and burned to death in the yard of the army clothing depot. For them and others who perished in that catastrophe a memorial building in reinforced concrete was later erected on the spot and a small Japanese garden laid out. It may console the spirit of the departed, and such a belief is a great consolation to the bereaved.

150

APPROACH TO HOFU-SO INN, TOKYO. The entrance gate was built near the left corner and the approach to the front door leads one to the right making a long approach and thereby adding dignity to the setting of the Inn. Not only the shape and size of the rocks are considered, but also their colour and texture in order to derive the greatest possible effect from them. Having been lately planted, the trees here are still propped up as protection against the wind.

151

ROJI OF THE HEAD-HOUSE OF MIYAKO SENKE, TOKYO. The *chaseki*, covered bench and other accessory buildings of the head-house of Miyako Senke Ceremonial Tea, were designed and constructed by Kimura Seibei, a famous *sukiya* style architect, who died recently. He also directed the layout of the garden, or *roji*. Miyako Senke is a new style of *chanoyu* originated by Miss Moriyama.

MR INOUYE'S WATER BASIN, TOKYO. The sound of falling water is one of the important elements in Japanese gardens especially in the *chaseki* garden. The amount of water allowed to run and the height of the bamboo pipe from which the water falls may be adjusted to obtain just the right tone. Not only is the music important, but also the significance of the fresh water which is used in washing hands and rinsing the mouth before entering the *chaseki* to partake of tea. Symbolically, anything of vice or meanness in the mind should be washed off so that one may enter with a clean and peaceful mind.

153

A BAMBOO GARDEN AT IMAMIYA SHINTO SHRINE. A simple tiny garden, such as this one cared for by Mr Sasaki at Murasakino gives endless pleasure to watch: there is the changing light and shadow on the moss-covered ground: or sometimes without even the breath of wind and in a perfect silence you may be awakened from a siesta by a sound ever so slight and wonder what it was that made the sound. Perhaps it was caused by a tiny creature, a frog jumping into the pond, the same sound which caused a priest a flash of inspiration, an enlightenment. But it may have been caused by mere passing of time.   Or as it may be, as an eighth-century Japanese poet sang in 753:

> 'Through the little bamboo bush
> Close to my chamber,
> The wind flows faintly rustling
> In this evening dusk.'

1. Front gate
2. Entrance to the house
3. Lawn
4. Pond (Old duck-hunting pond)
5. Tea room

THE HAPPO-EN, TOKYO. Until about 1954 a pine-tree more than 300 years old which was said to have been planted when Okubo Hikozaemon, the famed vizier lived here, thrived in this garden.

The garden was laid out on a hillside which slopes down to a natural pond fed by springs. After entering a stately gate-house, the entrance to the house is partially concealed. It is an excellent example of a Japanese-style house in its intimate relation to nature. There are many large pines, *muku* (*Aphananthe aspera*), etc. It has a rock composition of a cataract on the slope to the east side of the pond. It also has a *chaseki* and a 13-storey stone stupa of ancient Kudaar standing among clipped azalea bushes. Since the last war the place has been run as a restaurant.

Area about 10 acres.

155

OPPOSITE: GARDEN OF MATSUZAWA ASYLUM, TOKYO. Professor Fusajiro Kato, of Keio University, soon after he joined the medical staff of the Matsuzawa Asylum, conceived the idea of making a beautiful Japanese-style garden as a form of occupational therapy. He chose for the garden site a flat piece of ground near the centre of the farmland of about 50 acres which was allotted for the asylum. The work was started and carried on enthusiastically by about a hundred inmates at a time, under the supervision of the head nurse Norizo Maeda, an experienced social reform worker. The main part of the work consisted of digging a large pond with hoe and shovel, carrying earth in straw-rope nets by means of a pole in teams of two, and piling it up in the middle of the pond as a mountainous island. In about three years the pile of earth reached a great height in the general shape of Fuji Mountain. But the disastrous earthquake which played havoc in the area in 1923 shook the top portion of the tall conical mountain into the pond, thus forming peninsulas and inlets. Nature has re-modelled the man-made landscape to look more natural. Then came a gardener named Eto, who had been the head gardener of Count Okuma's garden at Waseda University. He was wise and left the island and pond as nature had re-modelled them and directed the work of beautifying the garden by planting trees.

INOKASHIRA PARK, TOKYO has from ancient times been famous for excellent natural springs which tea-devotees made very much of. Even before modern means of communication, some people came here from miles to get a bottle of water to take home and use in *chanoyu*. The place became very famous when the Kanda Josui water system was established for the people of Edo. Later when the Tamagawa Josui was established, it was used as a reservoir. In this lake there are several natural springs which never dry. Tokugawa Iyemitsu, the third Shogun, on one of his hunting trips quenched his thirst by one of the springs and felt so grateful that he dedicated a new building to the Benten shrine.

GARDEN OF MATSUZAWA ASYLUM TOKYO

About 700 inmates participated in the work of the garden during the six years of its construction, all having enjoyed the work. No less than sixty of them regained their sanity by this 'treatment' which brought them into direct contact with nature.

In the conclusion to *Gardens of Japan* I referred to this interesting experiment. I had the pleasure of visiting the garden a few days ago and of being able to include in this volume one or two photographs.

CONCLUSION

The conclusion I arrived at twenty-seven years ago when *Gardens of Japan* was published holds true today. As I then observed, the gardens of Japan, made according to their traditional ideal, are too deeply rooted to wither away under the glare of western influence. Since that time some of the salient features of our garden have indeed come to be better known and appreciated by the world.

Throughout history, the garden has constituted a part of our national life, and revealed our taste and characteristics. To be sure, its actual making and the ideals governing it, have changed slightly from time to time having been influenced by the prevailing thoughts of each period. Yet the fundamental ideals have remained firm and essentially unchanged.

The appreciation in the garden of the elusive quality in the art and conduct of men known as *shibumi*, *wabi* or *sabi*, remains very strong. These three terms are synonyms used according to different circumstances. They refer to an aesthetic quality indispensable to real art. They express the exact opposite of anything gaudy or ostentatious. They refer to the quality which has been greatly developed since the introduction of the Zen sect of Buddhism into Japan in the twelfth century. It is quiet and subdued; it is natural and has depth, but avoids being too apparent or ostentatious. It is simple without being crude; austere without being severe. It is the refinement that gives spiritual joy; a subtle touch of modesty of the soul. Our tea ceremony which is an institution founded upon the adoration of beauty amid the sordid facts of everyday life, may be said to be heavily charged with this quality.

Shibumi indeed is found in the moss covering the ground, in the rocks, stone lanterns and water-basins in the garden. It is revealed in the story of what Rikyu did when his son swept the garden. He told his son to tidy up the garden one day when he was expecting guests. When the son reported that his task was done, his father was not satisfied, and told him to try again. After a while he returned and said to his father that he had swept the garden three times, and not a dead twig or stray straw was to be found anywhere and that the garden was well sprinkled with water and that there was nothing more for him to do.

'You little idiot, just watch me!' rebuked the father, and quickly stepped along the stepping-stones to a maple-tree and shook it (it happened to be early in autumn), scattering gold and crimson leaves over the ground covered with green moss. 'There,' said the great master, pointing to the wonderful brocade thus created, 'that is the way to sweep the garden path!'

We still strive to satisfy our yearning for Nature in our gardens, not stopping merely at creating and arranging beautiful spots, but aiming at re-creating nature so that the garden may give peace and refreshment to men, and be a fitting abode in which the soul can rest and find spiritual refreshment.

158

GLOSSARY

Amida: Buddha having his paradise in the West where the faithful may be reborn.

Bodhisattva (Bosatsu) are almost Buddha, but not quite.

Boseki: a branch of art which developed in the Muromachi period. It depicts landscape with small stones and sand on a black lacquered tray, used as a decoration in the house.

Buddha: enlightened or perfect. Being so he requires no personal ornaments, no crown, no pendants etc.

Buddhist Trinity: the most common trinity is Amida trinity, with Amida in the middle attended by Kannon and Seishi on either side; another is Shakamuni trinity, with Shakamuni in the middle and attended by Monju and Fugen.

Chanoyu: commonly translated as tea ceremony, but it is an institution founded upon the adoration of beauty in the routine of everyday life.

Chaseki: small house or room for *chanoyu*.

Chisen-kaiyu-shiki: garden with pond to be appreciated by sauntering. *Chisen* means pond and spring or stream; and *kaiyu* means sauntering; *shiki* is type or style.

Chisen-kansho-shiki: garden with pond to be appreciated from a given point in the house, generally from the study.

Chisen-shu-yu-shiki: garden with pond to be enjoyed from a boat moving about in the pond.

Crane: symbolic of long life; believed to live for 1,000 years.

-en (suffix): hermitage, used for arbours, small temples, and *chaseki* (q.v.).

Fudo myoo: Acala, a fierce-looking messenger of Buddha symbolized in the garden by a waterfall. This deity is generally attended by two boys.

Fujito-seki: a rock which was first in the garden of the Hosokawa mansion, then taken to the garden of the Nijo Castle, then to Hideyoshi's Juraku villa, then to the Sanbo-in garden where it remains.

Gogyo: the ancient conception of the five elementary forces: wood, fire, earth, metal and water.

Gojo: five cardinal virtues: *jin* humanity, *gi* justice, *rei* politeness, *chi* wisdom, *shin* fidelity.

Hira niwa: level garden.

Hojo: literally ten-foot cubic dwelling in which Vimalakint (Buddhist saint) was believed to have lived. The term came to designate the front part of the temple.

Honsho ribetsu: a warning that a plant which grows in the heart of a high mountain should not be planted by the pond, or the plant which grows by the pond should not be planted on the hill-top.

Horai: an imaginary island shaped like a tortoise in the ocean where immortals were believed to dwell. Symbolized in a rock composition and auspicious of long life; the origin traced to Taoism.

In Yo: negative and positive principles in this universe; male and female principles, the creating forces of the universe.

-In: a building in temple precinct.

-Ji: temple (Buddhist).

Jinsha: shrine (Shinto).

Jizo: a Bodhisattva; children's deity, trying to keep human aspiration to become Buddha ever alert.

Kairaku: pleasure shared with their people.

Kare Sansui: dry landscape garden.

Koraku: after-pleasure. Often used as the name of a park or garden. Taken from a Chinese quotation: the wise feudal lord should worry before his people begin to worry; and have pleasure after his people have enjoyed.

Kasyapa: one of Shakamuni's disciples who smiled before his teacher spoke, and the teacher knew that he understood him. A communication of one mind to another.

Kudara: Paekche, a Korean kingdom which existed from A.D. 372–663.

Kuden: denoting a transmission by the mouth; a thing not to be written down but to be transmitted from mouth to the ear. In this context, secrets in the art of garden construction.

Kyokusui: winding stream.

Mandara of the nine realms of Amida's paradise: refers to the symbolic representation of Amida's Pure Land which is believed to be divided into three sections, each containing three realms of upper, middle and lower where souls are to be reborn according to the merit each person has achieved.

Manyoshu: oldest Japanese anthologies containing in all 4,516 verses written for the most part by poets who flourished in the seventh and eighth centuries.

Ming: Chinese dynasty (1368–1644).

Niwashi: gardeners.

Raja: generals who are guardians of Buddhism against evil spirits.

Rakan: Buddhist saints suggested in gardens by groups of rocks. In art they are generally represented either in 16 or 500.

159

Roji: garden paths to tea rooms. The term literally means 'dew ground' or 'dew path' said to have been taken from Buddhist *sutra* (sacred writing) which speaks of men being born in the 'dewy ground' free from the 'fiery abode of avarice'. It is a type of garden. Though actually very small as a garden, some *roji* give the feeling of mystic profundity and tranquillity.

Sabi: see *shibumi*.

Sanyu: the three friends in cold winter, referring to the plum-tree, daffodil and bamboo.

Sawa-tobi or **Sawa-watari:** stepping stones laid in water.

Sekimori-ishi: a cobblestone tied with bracken-fern rope indicates that the passage is closed. The name indicates that the stone stands for the caretaker of the barrier.

Seven lucky gods: Shichifuku-jin: Ebisu, Daikoku, Bishamonten, Benten, Fukurokuju, Jurojin and Hotei Osho.

Shakkei: borrowed natural scenes or objects from outside of the garden.

Shibumi, wabi, sabi: three terms synonomous of an aesthetic quality indispensable to real art. See page 158.

Shime-Nawa: a rope with tufts of rice straw or paper twisted at fixed intervals in proper sequence of 7, 5 and 3; it is hung in front of the shrine in order to sanctify the place within.

Shochiku-bai: pine, bamboo and plum; an auspicious group of these three species of plants was sometimes planted in a garden.

Shogun: war lord.

Shoin: guest room or study.

Shoin zukuri: *shoin* style architecture which provided a *tokonoma*, an alcove for hanging a painting, a window with built-in table for writing and study.

Shinden zukuri: symmetrical style architecture developed about the tenth to eleventh centuries.

Shukkei: gardens which reproduced a scene reduced in scale.

Shumisen: the central mountain of every world. Its origin is in Hindu cosmology, which existed there before Buddhism took it over. Later it became mixed with Horai ideas.

Stupa: pagoda, sacred tower.

Southern Sung: Chinese dynasties, 1127–1280.

Sukiyaki: a Japanese style of cooking thinly sliced beef with vegetables in a pan over charcoal fire over a brazier, seasoned with soy sauce. Beef may be substituted by chicken or duck.

Suteishi: 'thrown away' rocks; so named when rocks are used apparently not for their own selves, but to emphasize the value of something else, or to create a certain desired atmosphere.

Taki-ishi: a kind of granite with crackled appearance found in Noto Peninsula.

Tango: one of the five festivals of the year, this being for boys observed on the 5th day of the 5th month.

-Tei: arbour.

Ten-chi-jin: Heaven, earth and man in their relative positions.

Tenno: Emperor when on the throne. When he abdicates he becomes Joko and may continue to rule.

Tortoise: symbol of a long life, being traditionally believed to live for 10,000 years.

Tsuki-Yama: artificial hills, usually built with earth dug up, in creating a pond.

Tsukubai: stone water basin for washing hands before entering the *chaseki*, a symbolic gesture to cleanse oneself internally as well as externally.

Wabi: see *Shibumi*.

Yüan: Chinese dynasty, 1280–1368.

Yugen: mystery: applied to gardens, the hidden meaning behind the external layout. Simplification and suggestion. See page 37.

Yukimi: one of the types of stone lanterns, the name suggests snow viewing, and it goes well with snow-covered landscape: generally placed close to the pond, for its reflection in water is charming.

Zen: a sect of Buddhism introduced into Japan in the twelfth century. It has influenced Japanese thoughts and nearly all branches of art, including gardens, paintings, *chanoyu* etc.

Date Due